DID CHRISTIANITY REPLACE JUDAISM?

DID CHRISTIANITY REPLACE JUDAISM?

The Problem of Supersessionism

Alan C. Mitchell

Paulist Press
New York / Mahwah, NJ

Cover image: by Mobilee/Depositphotos.com
Cover design by Sharyn Banks
Book design by Lynn Else

Library of Congress Cataloging-in-Publication Data
Names: Mitchell, Alan C. author
Title: Did Christianity replace Judaism? : the problem of supersessionism / Alan C. Mitchell.
Description: Paperback. | New York: Paulist Press, [2025] | Includes bibliographical references and index. | Summary: "An introduction for general readers to supersessionism or replacement theology in New Testament interpretation, and how harmful it is to Christian/Jewish relations"—Provided by publisher.
Identifiers: LCCN 2025015927 (print) | LCCN 2025015928 (ebook) | ISBN 9780809155439 paperback | ISBN 9781587689413 ebook
Subjects: LCSH: Catholic Church—Relations—Judaism—History—20th century | Judaism (Christian theology) | Jews—Election, Doctrine of | Judaism--Relations--Christianity | Christianity and other religions—Judaism | Christianity and antisemitism | Bible. New Testament—Theology | Church—History of doctrines—Early church, ca. 30–600
Classification: LCC BT93 .M58 2025 (print) | LCC BT93 (ebook) | DDC 231.7/6—dc23/eng/20250909
LC record available at https://lccn.loc.gov/2025015927
LC ebook record available at https://lccn.loc.gov/2025015928

ISBN 978-0-8091-5543-9 (paperback)
ISBN 978-1-58768-941-3 (ebook)

Published by Paulist Press
997 Macarthur Boulevard
Mahwah, NJ 07430
www.paulistpress.com

Printed and bound in the
United States of America

For Julia and Aidan

Deus semper maior

CONTENTS

PREFACE

Supersessionism, the theology that holds that Judaism was replaced by Christianity, has been around for a long time, in fact since the second century CE. It has a long history and has contributed to anti-Judaism and antisemitism, but to be properly understood it should not be conflated with those. Supersessionism is both a theological position and a mindset that assumes one or more of the following: that the very idea of Christianity has made Judaism obsolete, that Jewish Scripture has no meaning apart from the Christian New Testament, that God's election of Israel and God's covenant with Israel were canceled with the coming of Jesus Christ, and that Jews were cursed by God to wander the earth until he comes again.

There is a reason for the subtitle of this book: *The Problem of Supersessionism*. The problem is manifold, it has proven pernicious, and it remains with us today. Christian supersessionism is a problem ?because it promotes both a distorted view of Judaism and a distorted self-understanding among Christians. It is a problem because of the damage it has done to the relationship between Judaism and Christianity, two religions that share so much in their history, tradition, rituals, and customs; they are kindred to each other, but the supersessionist perspective attempts to nullify that relationship. Finally, it is a problem because it has served as a rationale for antisemitism as it has also been fueled by it. As a mindset, it was a contributing factor to the *Shoah*, the Hebrew word for catastrophe, which Christians call the *Holocaust*. While it is true that the two hundred rabbis and intellectuals who signed the statement "*Dabru Emet*: A Jewish Statement on Christians and Jews" did not identify National Socialism as a Christian phenomenon, it is also true that the implementation of anti-Jewish laws and of the Final Solution was enabled by Christians. Since the Second Vatican Council in the 1960s, the Roman Catholic Church has unequivocally rejected supersessionism.

I have written this book to help people understand the problem, to argue that supersessionism is not intrinsic to Christianity, and to persuade Christians to reject supersessionism unequivocally. As a Scripture scholar, my main task is to argue that the texts of the New Testament are not supersessionist and that Christian supersessionist theologies emerged in the second century. In the first chapter, "The Problem of Supersessionism," I begin by explaining how the followers of Jesus did not see themselves as belonging to a group that had replaced Judaism. Jesus, his apostles, disciples, and followers were Jews and saw themselves as a part of Judaism. For that reason, they would be more properly called *Jesus Messianists*—Jews who recognized Jesus as the Messiah. I go on to describe supersessionism in some detail. And then I examine an early supersessionist text, the *Epistle of Barnabas* from the early second century CE, using that to illustrate what supersessionism looks like and laying forth its basic principles.

In the second chapter, "Is the New Testament Supersessionist?," I address the charge by some scholars who think that there is an incipient form of supersessionism already at home in certain New Testament books—for example, the letters of Paul, the Gospels of Matthew and John, and the Letter to the Hebrews. I answer the question in the negative through a close reading of the most problematic passages within those texts. Here I am in close conversation with other New Testament scholars who also reject supersessionist interpretations. The point is a crucial one: Christianity is not inherently supersessionist.

In the third chapter, "The Advent of Christian Supersessionism in the Second Century and Its Later Growth," I trace the beginnings of supersessionist thought to certain second-century Christian authors. I examine the *Epistle to Diognetus* and other works by second-century apologists (such as Justin Martyr, Irenaeus of Lyons, and Melito of Sardis) as they tried to make the case for the rational and moral legitimacy of Christianity. I then turn to the fourth century, after Christianity was legalized and became the dominant religion of the Roman Empire. I look at Syrian Antioch and the eight discourses *Against the Judaizing Christians*, composed and preached by John Chrysostom. I conclude with a brief examination of the *Adversus Judaeos* (*Against the Jews*) tradition and its intensifying supersessionism from the fourth century to the Middle Ages.

In the fourth and final chapter, "Roman Catholic Teaching on Supersessionism," I focus on the twentieth century. I begin with an overview of how the anti-Judaism, antisemitism, and supersessionist mindset of the first half of that century contributed to the catastrophic extermination of six million Jews under National Socialism in the Shoah. In the remainder of the chapter, I show how the effects of that catastrophe were the catalyst for a seismic change among Christian churches, particularly the Roman Catholic Church, where finally anti-Jewish hate, antisemitism, and supersessionism were unequivocally condemned. I argue that that seismic change came about in no small part because of advances in biblical scholarship and the Church's embrace of the historical-critical method in 1943—and thus its rejection of older typological and allegorical interpretations that had fed supersessionism throughout the centuries. Finally, I conclude by describing the many efforts by the Church and Catholic scholars to repair the damage to Jewish-Christian relations caused by so many centuries of animosity toward Jews.

My hope is that together these chapters will inform readers of the nature of the problem of supersessionism and its scope in history and will also establish in their minds that Christianity is not inherently supersessionist. Seeing actual examples of supersessionism will hopefully increase awareness of its consequences and sensitize readers to its effects. That is the bad news part of the book. There is good news as well. Christians and Jews reached a turning point in the post-Shoah era. For Roman Catholics, there was a seismic shift away from supersessionism with the promulgation of *Nostra Aetate* at the Second Vatican Council in 1965. *Nostra Aetate* strongly condemned supersessionism along with its accompanying anti-Judaism and antisemitism as well as any form of discrimination against Jews. Since then, through several joint initiatives, Jews and Christians have acknowledged their differences honestly and are able to celebrate what they have in common. More than that, Christianity thrives best in recognizing its deep roots in Judaism, in respecting Judaism and Jews, and in engaging in dialogue and common enterprises. Seeking mutual dialogue and collaboration is now commonplace among Christians and Jews; established institutes, consultations and dialogues facilitate those exchanges. Division has been replaced by cooperation. That notwithstanding, there has been a rise in global antisemitism among Christians in recent years. In 2017 at Charlottesville, Virginia, white supremacists chanted "Jews will not replace us." A year later, eleven people were killed in a shooting at the Tree of Life synagogue in Pittsburgh, PA. In the United States, the Christian nationalist movement is growing. The hope is that education and raising awareness of antisemitism and its effects can curb that trend, as can dialogue and collaboration among Christians and Jews. There is still much to accomplish, and it is my hope that this book will be a helpful contribution to that purpose.

While writing a book can be a lonely endeavor, no one writes a book alone. There are so many people who have helped me to bring this book to completion. I want to thank my colleagues, students, and friends, both Christian and Jewish, who have taught me much that I needed to learn about why supersessionism is the problem that it is. I cannot name everyone, but I do want to thank my initial editor at Paulist Press, Christopher Bellitto, for his guidance and suggestions in shepherding this project toward its goal. I want to acknowledge especially Donna Crilly, Senior Academic Editor, for her magnificent editorial attention to and suggestions for refining my manuscript. I am grateful, as well, to the staff at Paulist Press for the work they have done on the book's production. I owe a debt of gratitude to my Georgetown colleagues: Leo Lefebure, for sharing his wisdom and insights on the problem of supersessionism and for reading the manuscript and offering very helpful suggestions for improving it; and John Borelli, who got the ball rolling when he invited me to deliver a paper on supersessionist interpretation of Hebrews at *Jewish-Catholic Relations: Interpreting Scripture and Current Self-Understanding*, a conference he organized at Georgetown in 2010; and Dr. Carole Sargent, Director of the Office of Scholarly Publications at Georgetown University for her invaluable help in securing the copyright permissions for the early Christian texts I have cited in this book. I want to remember the late Gerard Mannion, who asked me to offer a paper on migration in Hebrews in honor of another Georgetown colleague, Peter Phan. It was at that conference that Christopher Bellitto asked me to write this book for Paulist Press. I must also thank Reverend Nicholas Austin, SJ, Master of Campion Hall at Oxford University and the Jesuits and staff there, for their warm hospitality and mirth. Finally, I thank the two people to whom this book is dedicated: my wife, Professor Julia Lamm, who has carefully read through the manuscript, offered excellent feedback, and helped me to put the book into its final form, and our son Aidan for his encouragement and humor. Together they have sustained me with their love, support, and advice, without which I could not have brought this project to completion. They also put up with me through the process of getting it done.

Alan C. Mitchell
Campion Hall, Oxford
July 25, 2024

Chapter One

THE PROBLEM OF SUPERSESSIONISM

It is a commonplace among scholars of religion that first-century Judaism was not a monolith. The earliest Christians were one emerging group among a variety of Judaisms. Jesus was a Jew, as were all his early followers. Jesus was born a Jew, circumcised on the eighth day according to Jewish custom, instructed in the Law and the Prophets, was a disciple of an apocalyptic Jewish preacher, John the Baptist, and a frequent dialogue partner with other Jews over matters of Sabbath observance and the practice of the Torah. Jesus resided in Galilee and gathered disciples from its environs, as other Jewish teachers had. He preached the coming reign of God, which he often described in parables and sayings, forms of Jewish Wisdom. In addition to preaching and teaching, he healed people's illnesses and infirmities, attending to the blind and the lame. He cast out demons, making people whole again. He was sometimes critical of Jewish authorities and of the way the Jerusalem Temple was administered, something for which the Romans executed him by crucifixion.

Jesus's death did not deter his disciples from continuing his mission to Israel. After the experience of his resurrection, his followers continued to identify as Jews. They can only be properly understood as one emerging group out of several others—Sadducees, Pharisees, Essenes, and Zealots. To remind us of the Jewish roots of these earliest Christians and of their belief in Jesus as the Messiah, modern scholars beginning in the eighteenth century identified them as "Jewish Christians." More recently, however, that designation has been deemed problematic. Carlton Paget in "Jewish Christianity" has discussed the many problems scholars have faced in attempting to offer a precise definition of "Jewish Christianity" and "Jewish-Christian."[1] For example, does the term refer to Jews who have converted to Christianity or can it include Gentiles who have become followers of Jesus?[2] According to Paget, one defining characteristic that set Jewish Christians apart from non-Christian Jews was their belief that Jesus Christ was the Messiah.[3] That is why I choose to call them *Jesus Messianists*, a term I borrow from Brendan Byrne, SJ.[4] This term describes these early followers of Jesus aptly as messianic Jews in the first century CE. The term also helps distinguish them from sectarian Jewish groups in their day that did not believe that Jesus was the Messiah.

JESUS MESSIANISTS

As Jews, the Jesus Messianists continued to practice their Judaism by attending the synagogue and observing the Sabbath. Their Scripture was that of Hellenistic Jews, the Septuagint, the Greek translation of Jewish Scripture. When New Testament authors quoted or alluded to Scripture, they always used the Septuagint, which they took as authoritative. In other words, there was no separate Scripture. Jesus Messianists also shared a communal meal, typical among the Jews of their day; they called this "The Lord's Supper," but they celebrated it on Sunday, which was for them the first day of the week. One assumes that they shared in the practice of Torah observance, although it is difficult to determine exactly what form that observance took. For example, the Sermon on the Mount in Matthew's Gospel and the Sermon on the Plain in Luke's alike present Jesus as an interpreter of Torah, at least for the communities associated with those Gospels. In both sermons, Jesus recognizes the Jewish law as authoritative and worthwhile. In Matthew, he clearly says that he has not come to abolish the law but to fulfill it, under a "new righteousness" (Matt 5:20). In other words, Matthew's Jesus does not replace the law or righteousness;

rather, he interprets both for his community in ways that embrace the law and righteousness in a Jewish context.

Still, Jesus Messianists were not monolithic in their Judaism, and so Jewish practices may have varied among them from one geographical region to another. If the account of the Jerusalem Council in Acts 15 is to be trusted, male Gentiles being initiated into Jesus Messianism were no longer required to be circumcised. The converts were instead enjoined to follow four Noahide laws—namely, abstention from meat that had been sacrificed to idols, abstention from the consumption of a sacrificial animal's blood, abstention from the consumption of a sacrificial animal that had been strangled and not ritually slaughtered, and finally, abstention from fornication (Acts 15:29). Against this compromise view stood those Jesus Messianists who went to the Pauline church in Galatia to convince Gentile converts that they had to submit to the rite of circumcision and observe Torah. Paul, a former Pharisee and a recent convert to Jesus Messianism, countered them, arguing that the Galatians who submit to circumcision are obliged to observe the entire law (Gal 5:3), but he denied that circumcision was necessary for Gentile converts because he saw them as being already a part of Israel (Gal 3:8). It also appears that the Jewish Jesus Messianists instructed the Galatians to follow a Jewish calendar governing Sabbaths, new moons, festival seasons, and sabbatical and jubilee years (Gal 4:10).

The Jewish War with Rome (70–73 CE) ended in the siege of Jerusalem and the destruction of the Temple. The Roman victory fundamentally altered Judaism in its various expressions. With the loss of the Temple and thus the cessation of sacrifice and priesthood, the aristocratic Sadducees lost their prominence. The Essenes disappeared when the Romans destroyed their compound at Khirbet Qumran. According to the Jewish historian Josephus, the Zealots committed mass suicide at the Herodian fortress of Masada (*The Jewish War*, 7.389–405). Only the Pharisees and the Jesus Messianists remained. The Pharisees would lay the foundation of Rabbinic Judaism. The Jesus Messianists managed to survive in cities where the movement had been already established, such as Antioch, Alexandria, and Rome. It is likely that they had fled Jerusalem during the War with Rome, although we do not have certain knowledge of that fleeing. Luke would have us believe that there had already been a dispersion of Jesus Messianists from Jerusalem after the persecution by Paul and the stoning of Stephen (Acts 8:1), but that scattering predated the establishment of the Pauline churches in which Jesus Messianism flourished and expanded to include Gentiles. In any case, after 73 CE there were two groups of sectarian Jews extant: the Pharisees and the Jesus Messianists.

The Gospels of Matthew and John, both written between 85 and 100 CE, provide evidence for tensions between Jesus Messianists and synagogue leaders, as we will examine more fully in chapter 2 below. It is likely that the Jesus Messianists' view of Jesus as their Messiah made their continued presence in synagogues problematic. Their proclamation of Jesus as the Son of God may also have called into question their monotheism. Consequently, the relationship of Jesus Messianists to non–Jesus Messianist Jews in these synagogues became strained.

The Jesus Messianists' practice of frequenting the synagogue as well as house churches seems to have been followed to the end of the first century CE, before there was any sharp distinction between Jesus Messianists and Pharisaic Jews. Sometime in the second century CE the rift between the two groups would become more apparent as Jesus Messianists began to define themselves over against non–Jesus Messianist Jews and vice versa. This process of definition eventually resulted in Christians distinguishing themselves from Jews and making exclusive claims that they represented a New Covenant with God as God's new chosen people, the spiritual Israel. The implication was that the Old Covenant was abrogated along with the election of Israel. Thus, we have the introduction of supersessionism in Christian theology, that is, a theology of replacement.

WHAT IS SUPERSESSIONISM?

Supersessionism is a replacement theology that rests on the view that, despite their common origin, Christianity has replaced Judaism. The etymology of the term *supersessionism* draws on the Latin words *super* ("above" or "on") and *sedere* ("to sit"). When a compound of the two words was formed, *supersedere*, it meant "to postpone" or "to defer." In the seventeenth century, the verb *to supersede* carried the added meaning of "to render void," "to annul," and "to replace," giving the replacement a higher status than what preceded it.[5] This development in the meaning of *to supersede* remains faithful to the original sense of the two Latin words, *super* and *sedere*, as "to place" something "above" something else. In Christian theology, *supersessionism* therefore came to refer to Christianity being placed above Judaism, thereby replacing it. Consequently, those Christian theologians who have assumed supersessionism insist not only that Judaism has been replaced but also that it has been annulled and rendered ineffective. They promote the idea that what God had originally promised to Israel was transferred to Christianity. In the end, Christians came to view the Church as the replacement of God's chosen people, the Jewish Law as replaced by Christ, and the Hebrew Bible as having no intrinsic value apart from the New Testament.

Types of Supersessionism

Whereas, in general, supersessionism espouses the belief that Christianity replaced Judaism, it has taken on several forms. In *The God of Israel and Christian Theology*, an excellent study on the topic, R. Kendall Soulen identifies three distinct kinds of supersessionism dating back to the second century of Christianity. (1) *Economic supersessionism* confines Israel's role in the history of salvation solely to prefiguring Christ. This form of supersessionism concludes that, with the coming of Christ, Israel's role in salvation history ceased to be relevant and has become obsolete. (2) *Punitive supersessionism* carries a retributive aspect to it by stressing the idea that God has punished Israel by taking the covenant away from it because it did not accept Christ. Thus, punitive supersessionism is more hostile to Judaism than economic supersessionism. Such hostility inevitably contributed to antisemitism. (3) *Structural supersessionism* deprives the Hebrew Bible of having an integrity of its own apart from the New Testament. Since the canon of Christian Scripture contains two testaments, the narrative of salvation must embrace both, which means that there is no place for a narrative of salvation for Jews in their Scripture alone. The meaning of Jewish Scripture is usurped in the Christian canon, leaving a narrative of salvation that can apply only to Christians. In other words, the narrative of salvation in the Hebrew Bible can only find fulfillment in the New Testament. Consequently, Hebrew Scripture has no independent valid role of its own as the sacred writ of Jews.[6]

Each of these types of supersession is detrimental to Judaism because each promotes the loss of something that is integral to Jewish identity. Economic supersession denies the value of Israel's history as the chosen people of God. Punitive supersessionism contests the claim that Israel's covenant with God is irrevocable. Structural supersessionism annuls the integrity of Jewish Scripture apart from the New Testament.

Supersessionism and Antisemitism

Another negative consequence of supersessionism is the specter of antisemitism. Antisemitism and supersessionism are two distinct, albeit related, phenomena. In his book *Polemic in the Book of Hebrews*, Lloyd Kim defines antisemitism as a prejudice directed toward Jews themselves, individually and as a people, precisely because they are Jews.[7] Antisemitism differs from supersessionism in that the latter is a *theological* position that promotes Christianity as a replacement for Judaism. According to Kim, neither position is acceptable, but it is important to keep the distinction in mind because people sometimes confuse them. While supersessionism is different from antisemitism, it has certainly contributed to it and in some cases is blatantly antisemitic, and antisemitism in turn can encourage supersessionist positions.

Kim's definition of *antisemitism*, however, may prove too simplified to stand up to historical scrutiny. Ivan Marcus in *How the West Became Antisemitic: Jews and the Formation of Europe, 800–1500* helpfully maps out current scholarly debates about antisemitism, including whether "antisemitism" can even be applied to premodern contexts. He summarizes the position of those who argue that antisemitism is a strictly modern phenomenon:

> Scholars like Hannah Arendt, who resisted using the term "antisemitism" for premodern Jew hatred, contended that the medieval centuries were thoroughly religious in assumptions and institutions, whereas modern antisemitism is grounded in assumptions that include secularism, nationalism, ideologies such as socialism and liberalism, and the pseudoscience of racist scientific assumptions about Jews.[8]

But then what do we call "premodern Jew hatred"? According to Marcus, "anti-Judaism" does not work because it carries "potentially exculpatory implications" for the Church.[9] To avoid, on the one hand, a *teleological view* that "sees a causal connection between medieval and modern forms of Jew hatred"[10] and, on the other hand, views that dissociate modern antisemitism from "premodern Jew hatred," Marcus recommends distinguishing between "medieval antisemitism" and "modern antisemitism";[11] presumably, "late antique antisemitism" would work, too. Moreover, this way of naming antisemitism while distinguishing among different historical forms that it took helps avoid the problem of anachronism.

Marcus identifies three stages of antisemitism.[12] In the earliest stage, which aligns with the primary focus of this book, he says that "Jews and Christians agreed that they lived in a *binary of inverted hierarchy*. Each thought that it should be above and control the other. Neither wanted to be subordinated to the other."[13] This first stage was that of a mutual rivalry as Judaism and Christianity, in their closeness, began to define themselves over against the other. The second stage emerged, he maintains, with the First Crusade at the end of the eleventh century, when "the structure of hierarchical power and chosenness was sharpened as Jews came to be seen as the dangerous enemy within."[14] And the third stage emerged in late medieval Europe when Jewish identity (especially older Jewish males) began to be assigned a "'racial' permanence."[15] According to Marcus, these three stages from the Middle Ages became, in effect, "three structural categories" that would be taken up and transformed by modern forms of antisemitism.[16] As he puts it, "This is the three-part structure that medieval and modern antisemitism share, even though the former has religious content and the latter is defined in modern terms."[17] Central to Marcus's argument overall is how, throughout this long period of time, whereas Jews typically directed their criticisms against Christianity as a *religion*, medieval Christians directed their criticisms of Judaism against *Jews*.[18]

In this book on supersessionism, I focus on what Marcus calls the first stage, that of a rivalry defined by a *binary of inverted hierarchy*. Unlike Marcus, however, I identify that stage as beginning not in the first century but in the second century CE, hence not in Paul's epistles or in the other books of the New Testament.[19] Like antisemitism (indeed, like all *-isms*), supersessionism has a long history and took on various forms. Nevertheless, it has some basic structural features. In the remaining part of this chapter, I begin to define those structural features. I offer by way of contrast an example of a noncanonical text (that is, a text that was circulated for a while but never made it into the canon of the New Testament) that is supersessionist. Through a close study of the *Epistle of Barnabas* from the early second century, I delineate basic supersessionist tenets and interpretive moves so that readers themselves may be able to identify later instances of supersessionism or, conversely, to recognize other texts as nonsupersessionist. This will serve to demonstrate the exegetical and theological moves that typify supersessionism and just how faulty they are. In chapter 2, I will then make the case for why the books of the New Testament are not supersessionist.

THE EXAMPLE OF THE EPISTLE OF BARNABAS

A look at the *Epistle of Barnabas* will help make the above definitions and typologies more concrete. This epistle is a second-century document rife with supersessionist theology in its first seventeen chapters. Its author is anonymous, although the name of Paul's traveling companion and fellow missionary, Barnabas, has been assigned to it. For that reason, I will refer to the author either as "the author" or as Barnabas, with the understanding that Barnabas was not the actual author. There is a consensus among scholars that it was composed around the year 130 CE, during the reign of the Emperor Hadrian, who in 135 CE had expelled the Jews from Jerusalem. Hadrian renamed the city *Aelia Capitolina*, a combination of his own gentilic name, *Aelius*, and the name of the god *Jupiter Capitolinus*. Hadrian dedicated the city to Jupiter and built a temple for him on the site of the Jerusalem Temple, which had been destroyed in 70 CE. This historical context is critical for understanding the epistle.

One particular issue concerns the identity of the temple that was constructed on the site of the Jerusalem Temple. Reidar Hvalvik maintains that the author of *Barnabas* is probably referring to the temple of Jupiter, not the Jewish Temple, in 16.3–4:[20]

> 16.3. Moreover, he says again, "See, those who have destroyed this temple will themselves build it."
>
> 16.4. This is happening. For because of their war, it was destroyed by their enemies. And now the servants of the enemies will themselves rebuild it.

If indeed that is the case, then the building of a temple to a Roman god on this sacred site would have been profoundly offensive to Jews. Other scholars, however, suggest that Barnabas does not have a physical temple in mind but rather a spiritual one—namely, the Christian community. If that is the case, then the author adopted a supersessionist perspective in this letter.

Given the tenor of the time when it was written, it comes as no surprise that the *Epistle of Barnabas* would be strongly anti-Jewish. As we shall see in chapter 3, in the second century several Christian authors sought to distinguish sharply between Jews and Christians and to encourage the latter not to be like the former. Based on a variant reading in one manuscript that has "proselytes" instead of "newcomers," some scholars have speculated that the *Barnabas* author is trying to dissuade Christians from converting to Judaism. Finding that evidence too scant, other scholars propose instead that the author is trying to convince Christians not to be like Jews. He seems to say as much in at least two passages early in the epistle:

> 2.9. And so, since we are not ignorant, we should perceive the good intention of our Father. For he is speaking to us, wanting us to seek how to make an offering to him without being deceived like them [the Jews].
>
> 3.6. The one who is patient anticipated, brothers, that the people he prepared in his beloved would believe, in a state of innocence. And so he revealed all things to us in advance, that we not be dashed against their law as newcomers [Or: proselytes].

The first text (2.9) is part of an argument beginning in chapter 2 that promotes the self-sufficiency of God as far as God has no need of "sacrifices, whole burnt offerings, or regular offerings" (2.4). The author buttresses this claim with a citation from Isaiah 1:11–13, from which he concludes, "And so he nullified these things that the new law of our Lord Jesus Christ, which is without the yoke of compulsion, should provide an offering not made by human hands" (2.6). The second text (3.6) is a warning against becoming Jewish converts, proselytes. Thus, Christians must not be like Jews.

Barnabas has twenty chapters, the first seventeen of which are clearly supersessionist in the way they present how the Jews, reading their Scriptures literally, have misunderstood them and their own Judaism. In what follows, I identify six tenets that the author proposes about the replacement of Judaism by Christianity, and I trace the interpretive moves he makes. These tenets and their rationalization will become typical of supersessionist theologies. In them, we can recognize all three of Soulen's types of supersessionism—economic, punitive, and structural—and how they function. The six tenets are:

1) *The Jews have lost their covenant (punitive supersessionism):*

> *Epistle of Barnabas* 4.6–8
>
> 6. And so you should understand. And yet again, I am asking you this as one who is from among you and who loves each

> and every one of you more than my own soul: watch yourselves now and do not become like some people by piling up your sins, saying that the covenant is both theirs and ours.
>
> 7. For it is ours. But they permanently lost it, in this way, when Moses had just received it. For the Scripture says, "Moses was on the mountain fasting for forty days and forty nights, and he received the covenant from the Lord, stone tablets written with the finger of the Lord's own hand."
>
> 8. But when they turned back to idols they lost it. For the Lord says this: "Moses, Moses, go down quickly, because your people, whom you led from the land of Egypt, has broken the law." Moses understood and cast the two tablets from his hands. And their covenant was smashed—that the covenant of his beloved, Jesus, might be sealed in our hearts, in the hope brought by faith in him.

The author here counters the idea that the covenant belongs both to Jews and Christians (4.6), arguing instead that the Jews lost the covenant when Aaron made the Golden Calf (Exod 32:1–20), which resulted in Moses's smashing of the tablets on which the Decalogue was inscribed (Exod 32:19). In the author's view, that destruction of the tablets put an end to the Jewish covenant. Consequently, the covenant of Jesus was inscribed on the hearts of Christians (4.8) as a punishment for the Jews.

The author thus casts an historical interpretation of the Exodus story aside for an allegorical one. In fact, the covenant was not "permanently" lost at that moment, as the author of *Barnabas* suggests. Rather, it was remade two chapters later in Exodus 34:1–28 according to the command God gave to Moses in 34:1: "The LORD said to Moses, 'Cut two tablets of stone like the former ones, and I will write on the tablets the words that were on the former tablets, which you broke.'"

2) *Christians have inherited the Jewish covenant (economic supersessionism):*

> *Epistle of Barnabas* 13.1–6 (see also 6.19; 9.9)
>
> 1. Now let us see whether it is this people or the first one

> that receives the inheritance, and whether the covenant is for us or them.
>
> 2. Hear what the Scripture says concerning the people, "Isaac prayed for Rebecca his wife, because she was infertile. And then she conceived." Then, "Rebecca went to inquire of the Lord, and the Lord said to her, 'There are two nations in your womb and two peoples in your belly, and one people will dominate the other and the greater will serve the lesser.'"
>
> 3. You ought to perceive who Isaac represents and who Rebecca, and whom he means when he shows that this people is greater than that one.
>
> 4. In another prophecy Jacob speaks more plainly to Joseph his son, when he says, "See, the Lord has not kept me from your presence. Bring your sons to me that I may bless them."
>
> 5. He brought Ephraim and Manasseh, wanting him to bless Manasseh since he was the elder. So Joseph brought him to the right hand of his father Jacob. But Jacob saw in the Spirit a type of the people who was to come later. And what does it say? "Jacob crossed his hands and placed his right hand on the head of Ephraim, the second and younger, and blessed him. And Joseph said to Jacob, 'Switch your right hand onto Manasseh's head, because he is my firstborn son.' Jacob said to Joseph, 'I know, my child, I know. But the greater will serve the lesser, and it is this one who will be blessed.'"
>
> 6. You see about whom he has decreed, that this people will be first, and the heir of the covenant.

The author reinterprets the Old Testament in such a way as to assert that the original heir of the covenant, Israel, has been replaced by Christianity. In 13.2, he retells the story of the origin of Israel and Edom (Gen 25:21–26), which predicts the enmity between the Israelites and the Edomites and how the latter will be subordinated to the former. Jacob, the younger son, represents the lesser one who will dominate the greater; hence, Esau must represent Judaism, who is then surpassed by Christianity. Whereas the historical and traditional Jewish interpretation always has Jacob representing Israel, Barnabas's allegorical and nonhistorical reading of the passage reassigns the roles in order to achieve the desired result that Christians are now the rightful heirs to the covenant.

A similar dynamic is evident in 13.4–6, where the story of Genesis 48:8–20 is recalled—namely, how the younger son, Ephraim, was placed over the older son, Manassah, when Jacob blessed them both. In the Genesis text, Jacob crosses his arms and places his right hand on the head of Ephraim so that the blessing would come to him, the younger of the two, instead of to the elder Manasseh, who should have been the rightful heir. *Barnabas* departs from the original account in claiming that *only* Ephraim is blessed (13.5). The effect is the subordination of the older son, Manasseh (Israel), to the younger son, Ephraim (Christianity). Therefore, the motif of the older serving the younger we have just seen in Genesis 25:21–26 is applied even more overtly here to emphasize the priority of Ephraim, representing Christianity, to which Manasseh, the older Israel, is subordinated. The author of *Barnabas* thus confirms the point in: "You see about whom he has decreed, that this people will be first, and the heir of the covenant" (2.6). "This people" here refers to Christianity, even though it is not older than Judaism. It must be noted that *Barnabas* has made a significant change in the Genesis text. In the Old Testament Ephraim is often equated with Israel (Isa 7:8, 17; 9:9; Jer 31:9), and in some instances the two terms are interchangeable (Hos 5:3; 6:4). *Barnabas*'s allegorical interpretation subordinates Manasseh to Ephraim, so that the latter is able to further the supersessionism that *Barnabas* promotes.

In chapter 8.7, the author of *Barnabas* introduces another standard trope of supersessionist theology: the deafness of Israel. He writes,

> And thus the things that have happened in this way are clear to us, but they are obscure to them, because they have not heard the voice of the Lord.

And so, the author intimates that Jews, in neglecting deeper allegorical meaning, have not accurately interpreted Scripture and thus have "not heard the voice of the Lord." This prepares his readers for what he will say in chapter 9, where he links being able to hear God correctly with a circumcised heart as opposed to an in-flesh circumcision. In other words, only an uncircumcised Christian can read Scripture accurately.

3) Circumcision is annulled (punitive supersessionism):

Chapter 9 focuses on the question of this correct hearing, by which the author means understanding Scripture metaphorically, allegorically, and figuratively. "Hearing" figures large in this chapter as a metaphor for interpreting Scripture as God intended it to be interpreted, with the guidance of the Spirit of the Lord. In other words, *Barnabas* denies the value of the literal sense (the plain meaning) of Scripture, which is how Jews supposedly understand their Scriptures. The author establishes the importance of correct hearing by assembling a chain of scriptural quotations, which in their historical sense call Israel to hear the word of the Lord, something that is a commonplace in the Hebrew Bible. *Barnabas*, however, changes the text to show God addressing Christians:

> *Barnabas* 9.1–4
>
> 1. For he speaks again about the ears, indicating how he has circumcised our hearts. The Lord says in the prophet, "They obeyed me because of what they heard with their ears" (Ps 18:44). Again he says, "Those who are far off will clearly hear; they will know what I have done" (Isa 33:13). And, "Circumcise your hearts" (Jer 4:4), says the Lord.
>
> 2. Again he says, "Hear O Israel, for thus says the Lord your God" (Jer 7:2–3; Ps 34:12–13). And again the Spirit of the Lord prophesies, "Who is the one who wants to live forever? Let him clearly hear the voice of my servant" (Isa 50:10; Exod 15:26).
>
> 3. Again he says, "Hear, O heaven, and give ear, O earth, for the Lord has said these things as a witness" (Isa 1:2). And again he says, "Hear the word of the Lord, you rulers

> of this people" (Isa 1:10; 28:14). And again he says, "Hear, O children, the voice of one crying in the wilderness" (Isa 40:3). Thus he circumcised our hearing, that once we heard the word we might believe.
>
> 4. But even the circumcision in which they trusted has been nullified. For he has said that circumcision is not a matter of the flesh. But they violated his law, because an evil angel instructed them.

To make matters worse, *Barnabas* avers that the literal understanding of Scripture does not originate with the Spirit of the Lord, but rather with an evil angel (9.4), thus attributing Jewish misunderstanding of Scripture to a demonic force. Circumcision initiates a Jewish male into the covenant with God and is a physical mark of that covenantal relationship, defining the identity of the Jewish male. In *Barnabas*, the metaphorical sense of circumcision in the Old Testament signifies that the outward physical sign of the covenant has been interiorized by the person bearing it—in other words, by the Christian. The author of *Barnabas* therefore destabilizes that physical sign. He reinterprets the Old Testament's metaphorical sense of circumcising the heart so that those who are not physically circumcised replace Israel, and he thereby redefines the identity of those in covenant with God. Remarkably, the author declares that since the correct understanding of circumcision "is not a matter of the flesh," Jewish circumcision has been annulled. Hence, the uncircumcised Christians replace the Jews.

This is another example of punitive supersessionism because the sign of what defined the Jewish male has been taken away and replaced by the exact opposite of that sign, now defining Christians as the heirs of the covenant. It is a punishment for Jews who have not heard the word of the Lord properly. The opening of the chapter serves to justify the author's method of interpreting Scripture allegorically. Nullifying the rite of circumcision is always evidence of supersessionist exegesis.

4) *The Old Testament is a Christian book (structural supersessionism):*

Barnabas 10.9 and 12

> 9. And so, Moses received the three firm teachings about food and spoke in the Spirit. But they received his words according to the desires of their own flesh, as if he were actually speaking about food.
>
> 12. But how could they know or understand these things? We, however, speak as those who know the commandments in an upright way, as the Lord wished. For this reason, he circumcised our hearing and our hearts, that we may understand these things.

After summarizing what Moses taught about food laws, the author indicates that Moses was not really talking about food. Citing examples taken from Leviticus and Deuteronomy of which animals can or cannot be eaten, thereby separating clean from unclean to remain ritually pure, *Barnabas* redirects the purpose of those laws to rules of behavior. The command not to eat pigs, he claims, is really a command not to associate with people who are like pigs as far as their life of luxury obscures their need for God. When Jews experience a hardship, they remember the Lord. When the pig is hungry it cries out to its master to feed it, but once it is fed it forgets its master and becomes silent once more (10.3). The author concludes, "So, then, the commandment of God is not a matter of avoiding food; but Moses spoke in the Spirit" (10.2). As seen in the above examples in which allegorical interpretation of Jewish Scripture favors a Christian typology, the examples in *Barnabas* 10 clearly reveal that the author of *Barnabas* has little regard for the historical meaning of those texts. He repeatedly shifts their meaning to an allegorical Christian interpretation of the Old Testament, suggesting that it was never intended to be Scripture for Jews.

For *Barnabas*, there is no other meaning apart from the exclusively Christian reading of Old Testament texts. What lessons Jews may have derived from their own Scripture have been supplanted by Christian typology. In 10.12, *Barnabas* directly engages the question of how Jews could possibly have understood their own Scripture. His answer is that Christians, whose hearts alone are circumcised, know the commandments of Scripture righteously, and therefore only they truly understand them. Such thinking is a clear example of structural supersessionism in which the canon of Scripture, now in two testaments, tells the history of salvation solely from a Christian point of view. According to this perspective, the entire Old Testament is prophecy that comes to an end in Jesus Christ. All other meanings are excluded. Jewish Scripture has been confiscated by Christianity and interpreted as though the Old Testament had no integrity of its own for the Jewish people.

5) *Christianity observes the Sabbath on the eighth day (punitive supersessionism):*

Barnabas 15.1–9

1. Something is also written about the Sabbath in the ten commandments, which God spoke to Moses face to face on Mount Sinai: "Make the Sabbath of the Lord holy, with pure hands and a pure heart."

2. In another place it says, "If my children keep the Sabbath, I will bestow my mercy on them."

3. This refers to the Sabbath at the beginning of creation: "God made the works of his hands in six days, and he finished on the seventh day; and he rested on it and made it holy."

4. Pay attention, children, to what it means that "he finished in six days." This means that in six thousand years the Lord will complete all things. For with him a day represents a thousand years. He himself testifies that I am right, when he says, "See, a day of the Lord will be like a thousand years." And so, children, all things will be completed in six days—that is to say, in six thousand years.

5. "And he rested on the seventh day." This means that when his Son comes he will put an end to the age of the lawless one, judge the impious, and alter the sun, moon, and stars; then he will indeed rest on the seventh day.

6. Moreover, it says, "Make it holy with pure hands and a pure heart." We are very much mistaken if we think that at the present time anyone, by having a pure heart, can make holy the day that the Lord has made holy.

> 7. And so you see that at that time, when we are given a good rest, we will make it holy—being able to do so because we ourselves have been made upright and have received the promise, when lawlessness is no more and all things have been made new by the Lord. Then we will be able to make the day holy, after we ourselves have been made holy.
>
> 8. Moreover he says to them, "I cannot stand your new moons and Sabbaths." You see what he means: It is not the Sabbaths of the present time that are acceptable to me, but the one I have made, in which I will give rest to all things and make a beginning of an eighth day, which is the beginning of another world.
>
> 9. Therefore also we celebrate the eighth day with gladness, for on it Jesus arose from the dead, and appeared, and ascended into heaven.

Beginning with the Sabbath rest described in the creation story and alluding to the command to observe it as a day of rest (Gen 2:2–3), the author adds a motivation not provided in the biblical text: it is to be observed with pure hands and a pure heart. Thus, faithful observance will elicit mercy from the Lord. Quickly the author leaves the Genesis account to interpret allegorically that six days really means six thousand years (Ps 90:4). With the introduction of the second coming of Christ (15.5) and the notice that it is impossible to make the Sabbath holy in the present age (15.6), the author concludes that the true Sabbath can only be observed at the end of the ages on an eighth day. In other words, it is Sunday that begins the age to come. He has abolished Jewish Sabbath observance and transferred it to a Christian eschatological Sabbath at the end of time.

6) *God brings Christians into his imperishable temple (punitive supersessionism):*

> *Barnabas* 16.1–10
>
> 1. I will also speak to you about the Temple, since those wretches were misguided in hoping in the building rather

than in their God who made them, as if the Temple were actually the house of God.

2. For they consecrated him in the Temple almost like the Gentiles do. But consider what the Lord says in order to invalidate it: "Who has measured the sky with the span of his hand or the earth with his outstretched fingers? Is it not I, says the Lord? The sky is my throne and the earth is the footstool for my feet. What sort of house will you build me, or where is the place I can rest?" You knew that their hope was in vain!

3. Moreover he says again, "See, those who have destroyed this temple will themselves build it."

4. This is happening. For because of their war, it was destroyed by their enemies. And now the servants of the enemies will themselves rebuild it.

5. Again it was revealed how the city, the Temple, and the people of Israel were about to be handed over. For the Scripture says, "It will be in the last days that the Lord will hand over to destruction the sheep of the pasture along with their enclosure and tower." And it has happened just as the Lord said.

6. But let us inquire if a temple of God still exists. It does exist, where he says that he is making and completing it. For it is written, "It will come about that when the seventh day is finished, a temple of God will be gloriously built in the name of the Lord."

7. And so I conclude that a temple exists. But learn how it will be built in the name of the Lord. Before we believed in God, the dwelling place of our heart was corrupt and feeble, since it really was a temple built by hand; for it was full of idolatry and was a house of demons, because we did everything that was opposed to God.

8. "But it will be built in the name of the Lord." Now pay attention, so that the temple of the Lord may be gloriously built. And learn how: we have become new, created again from the beginning, because we have received the forgiveness

> of sins and have hoped in the name. Therefore, God truly resides within our place of dwelling—within us.
>
> 9. How so? His word of faith, his call to us through his promise, the wisdom of his upright demands, the commandments of the teaching, he himself prophesying in us and dwelling in us who had served death, opening up to us the door of the temple, which is the mouth, and giving repentance to us—thus he brings us into his imperishable temple.
>
> 10. For the one who longs to be saved looks not merely to a person but to the one who dwells and speaks in him. For he is amazed at him since he has never heard him speak these words from his mouth nor even ever desired to hear them. This is a spiritual temple built for the Lord.

Since the author of *Barnabas* has transferred all the major institutions of Judaism to Christianity, it is unsurprising that he would take advantage of the destruction of the Second Temple to move that over to the Christian column as well. His treatment of the Temple begins with a consideration of how misguided Jews placed their hope in a building rather than in God alone, thus questioning whether the Temple was ever the actual house of God. In so doing, the author capitalizes on the debate over whether there should have been a Temple from the time when David expressed his desire to build a temple for God. Acknowledging that Solomon dedicated the Temple, the author quickly moves to establish that nonetheless God disqualified the Temple (16.2). Appealing to texts from Isaiah 40:12 and 66:1, which were written after the destruction of the First Temple by the Babylonians, *Barnabas* suggests that the universe is God's temple and that no earthly dwelling would suffice as the house of God. Although it is the case that the historical meaning of the first text (Isa 40:12) speaks to the incomprehensibility of God and how no human can fathom God's plan for creation, and that the second text (Isa 66:1) appears to suggest that God dwells in heaven and not on earth, it does not follow that these two texts "invalidate" an earthly temple, as the author suggests.

An historical reading of Solomon's dedication of the Temple

in 1 Kings 8 counters the spiritualized reading by the author of *Barnabas*. In his prayer Solomon first acknowledges the expansiveness of God. In 8:27 he says, "But will God indeed dwell on the earth? Even heaven and the highest heaven cannot contain you, much less this house that I have built!" In the remainder of the dedicatory prayer, Solomon describes reasons why humans will come to the Temple in good and bad times to pray and supplicate, and he asks that God in heaven hear their prayers:

> Hear the plea of your servant and of your people Israel when they pray toward this place; O hear in heaven your dwelling place; heed and forgive (1 Kgs 8:30).

The text, therefore, does not support *Barnabas*'s interpretation. By ignoring the historical meaning of these texts, the epistle undermines the importance of the Temple in Judaism in order to make room for his Christian spiritualization of the Temple. Thus, he has to establish that the physical Temple was an impermanent fabrication of Judaism that has disappeared. His is a tendentious use of history to further an anti-Jewish agenda, which is confirmed at the end of 16.2: "You knew that their hope was in vain!"

In 16.6 the author questions whether the temple of God still exists. At 16.7 he affirms that it does exist. He backs up the claim with what purports to be a scriptural verse, although it is not clear from where it comes. Two editors of the *Epistle of Barnabas* in the Loeb Classical Library, Kirsopp Lake and Bart Ehrman, suggest it comes from Daniel 9:24–27 and 1 Enoch 91:13. The text of Daniel, however, does not speak of building a temple; and 1 Enoch speaks of building a house for the Great King, who is presumably God, but the context suggests that it is an earthly temple. The author of *Barnabas*, however, takes it to be a spiritual temple "gloriously built in the name of the Lord" (16.6). That interiorized spiritual temple comes about through the process of conversion, as the author speaks about the corruption of the heart before one comes to believe in God, a heart described as "full of idolatry" and "a house of demons." Through baptism, the believer becomes a new creation, having received the forgiveness of sins and hope in the name of the Lord. Thus, God dwells in that temple of the converted heart, and so the temple that still exists is within the believer—that is within the Christian (16.8). As he makes clear in 16.9–10, it is a spiritual, interiorized temple.

In summary, *Barnabas*'s anti-Jewish stance tried to deprive Judaism of its important institutions. According to *Barnabas*, the covenant, circumcision, and ritual law, Scripture, Sabbath, and temple have all been stripped away from Judaism and handed over to Christianity. The author of *Barnabas* denies the integrity of Judaism and its major institutions, which is tantamount to denying that it is a legitimate religion. How is this denigration of Judaism possible? According to *Barnabas*, the denial of Judaism and its institutions is mandated by the correct reading of Scripture:

> 1.7 For through the prophets the Master has made known to us what has happened and what now is; and he has given us the first fruits of the taste of what is yet to be. And as we see that each and every thing has happened just as he indicated, we should make a more abundant and exalted offering in awe of him.

Reading Scripture as he does, allegorically and typologically, the author claims that the sacred text, read as prophecy, shows the true meaning of the past, the present, and the hope of the future. The outcome of his scriptural interpretation is anti-Jewish and offensive to Judaism. It is also supersessionist in the insidious way it undermines the validity of Judaism, its institutions, and the plain meaning of its Scriptures, and replaces it and them with Christianity.

CONCLUSION

It is not just the transference of those Jewish institutions to Christianity that is the problem. Supersessionism calls into question the veracity of God's promises to the Jewish people. This stands in contradiction to the Hebrew Bible, which extols God as eternally faithful to Israel and proclaims that the covenant is eternal. Within Judaism, infidelity to the covenant does not result in God's abandonment of the Jewish people. Quite to the contrary, God continually pursues Israel to offer reconciliation and forgiveness. The covenant between Israel and God is based on God's steadfast love which is never withdrawn. To present the Old Testament as simply the precursor to the New Testament, without any validity of its own, is a gross misrepresentation of Jewish Scripture. Furthermore, claiming that the Old Testament is fulfilled only in the New disregards God's promises and fidelity to Israel. Doing so disenfranchises Jews. Thus, the *Epistle of Barnabas* demonstrates the harm that a supersessionist interpretation of Scripture does to the people first chosen by God.

It is not only Judaism that suffers from the supersessionist misreading of Scripture, for Christianity suffers as well. When the link between the testaments is severed, Christianity loses the rich tradition and heritage that is the legacy it received from Judaism. The Apostle Paul catalogued that legacy in Romans 9:4–5:

> They are Israelites, and to them belong the adoption, the glory, the covenants, the giving of the law, the worship, and the promises; to them belong the patriarchs, and from them, according to the flesh, comes the Messiah, who is over all, God blessed forever. Amen.

And he proclaimed the permanence of that legacy in Romans 11:29: "For the gifts and the calling of God are irrevocable." When that legacy is sundered from its Jewish origin, it is appropriated in a way that suggests that it was always only intended to be a Christian legacy. Thus, the integrity of Christianity itself is challenged because supersessionism prevents the whole story of Christianity from being told. If the story of what God has done in Jesus Christ is not a continuation of what has done for Israel, Christian theology is impoverished, for so much of the story of salvation history cannot be fully told without understanding Israel and Judaism as an essential part of that story.

In its landmark document *The Jewish People and Their Sacred Scriptures in the Christian Bible* (2001), The Pontifical Biblical Commission repeatedly articulates the close relationship between the Old and the New Testaments as a sign of the close relationship between Judaism and Christianity. As stated clearly in the document's Preface and its first section:

> The question which is asked is the following: What relations does the Christian Bible establish between Christians and the Jewish people? The general answer is clear: between Christians and Jews, the Christian Bible establishes many close relations. Firstly, because the Christian Bible is composed, for the greater part, of the "Holy Scriptures" (Rm 1:2) of the Jewish people, which Christians call the "Old Testament"; secondly, because the Christian Bible is also comprised of a collection of writings which, while expressing faith in Christ Jesus, puts them in close relationship with the Jewish Sacred Scriptures. This second collection, as we know, is called the "New Testament", an expression correlative to "Old Testament" (Preface).
>
> Christianity, then, came to birth in the bosom of first century Judaism. Although it gradually detached itself from Judaism, the Church could never forget its Jewish roots, something clearly attested in the New Testament; it even recognized a certain priority for Jews, for the Gospel is the "power of God for salvation to everyone who has faith, *to the Jew first* and also to the Greek" (Rm 1:16). (Section 1.2)

The commission therefore makes clear what exactly is lost when supersessionism gets in the way of the relationship between Christianity and Judaism: the close relationship of Christianity and Judaism in the Scriptures they share and the rootedness of Christianity itself in Judaism.

Similarly, as we will investigate more fully in chapter 4 below, the Second Vatican Council's Declaration on the Relation of the Christian Church to non-Christian Religions (1965), denounces the supersessionist interpretation of Scripture and the antisemitism to which it gives rise:

> Although the Church is the new people of God, *the Jews should not be presented as rejected or accursed by God, as if this followed from the Holy Scriptures.* All should see to it, then, that in catechetical work or in the preaching of the word of God they do not teach anything that does not conform to the truth of the Gospel and the spirit of Christ.
>
> Furthermore, in her rejection of every persecution against any man, the Church, mindful of the patrimony she shares with the Jews and moved not by political reasons but by the Gospel's spiritual love, decries hatred, persecutions, displays of anti-Semitism, directed against Jews at any time and by anyone. (*Nostra Aetate* 4; italics mine)

It is as though the Council had *The Epistle of Barnabas* in mind.

We now turn to the texts that made it into the canon of the New Testament, especially those often misinterpreted in a supersessionist light. None of the six supersessionist tenets we found in the *Epistle of Barnabas*, nor any of those exegetical moves, are present in Paul's Epistles, Matthew, John, or Hebrews. On the contrary, what we find there are sophisticated arguments and exegesis from within Judaism that address debatable issues between Jesus Messianists and their Jewish confreres.

Chapter Two

IS THE NEW TESTAMENT SUPERSESSIONIST?

Addressing the question of whether or not Christianity is inherently supersessionist does not depend on first determining whether or when there was a definitive "parting of the ways"—a phrase that scholars use to refer to when, and how, Judaism and Christianity became identified as distinct religions. I maintain that, since supersessionism is a theological phenomenon, it can be studied apart from the historical question of when Christians left the matrix of Judaism. I argue in this chapter that the New Testament texts are not supersessionist.

Some interpreters have suggested that within the New Testament we can find evidence of an attempt to replace Judaism with Christianity. As examples of this early supersessionism, they offer Paul's letters, in particular Galatians and Romans, which were written in the 50s and 60s CE; and the Gospels of Matthew and John, written around 80–90 CE; and the Epistle to the Hebrews, written after 70 CE. In what follows, I closely examine those New Testament texts and demonstrate that, once understood in context, they are not supersessionist but instead provide evidence of the pluralistic context out of which Christianity emerged.

THE LETTERS OF PAUL

Was there already a degree of supersessionism as early as the "law-free" mission that the Apostle Paul preached to Gentiles (Gal 1:15–16; 2:7–8)? An affirmative answer would contradict Paul himself. Paul boasted of his Jewish heritage, suggesting that he still saw himself as a Jew (Phil 3:3–6). Even Luke, one of the first interpreters of Paul, in his Acts of the Apostles has Paul strongly identifying as a Jew (Acts 21:39, 23:3). What seems to have happened is that Paul transitioned from Pharisaic Judaism to Jesus Messianism after his experience of Jesus Christ while traveling on the road to Damascus—an experience that caused him to count his former life in Pharisaic Judaism as a loss (Phil 3:7–10). As strong as he was in making this claim, one must ask whether Paul was merely being rhetorical when he wrote that. In other words, could he have written it with hyperbole to emphasize the importance of the experience of Christ on the road to Damascus? It appears to simplify his relationship to Judaism, which was actually more complicated than conventional assumptions about his "conversion" from Judaism to Christianity have acknowledged. Thanks to Krister Stendahl in "The Apostle Paul and the Introspective Conscience of the West,"[1] scholars have become more nuanced in assessing Paul's experience of Christ on the road to Damascus (Gal 1:15–16), seeing it more as a prophetic call from God that set him apart for a particular purpose in his preaching about Christ than as a conversion to a "new religion." It seems actually to have been a deepening of his experiences as a Jew. Apparently, the loss Paul spoke of in Philippians 3:3–6 was not a total loss insofar as he did not leave Judaism completely; he simply moved to another sect of Judaism, which is to say, to Jesus Messianism. That sect was still within the Judaisms of Paul's day, and it was comprised of Jewish and Gentile believers who were followers of Jesus Christ.

Paul established a community of Jesus Messianists among Gentile believers in Galatia in Asia Minor sometime in the mid-50s of the first century CE. In his letter to them, he advanced a novel theory about how Gentiles could be incorporated into Jesus Messianism without formally becoming Jews. Prior to Paul, male

Gentiles wanting to enter Jesus Messianism first had to undergo the Jewish rite of circumcision and adhere to some of the Jewish Law (Acts 15:1–5). Paul's understanding of the way God declared Abraham as righteous in Genesis 15:6 focused on how Abraham believed that God would fulfill the promise he made to him in Genesis 12:1–3. As a result, God reckoned Abraham as righteous, being in right relationship to God, based on his faith in God. Since this reckoning had come before God made a covenant of circumcision with Abraham in Genesis 17, Paul concluded that, like Abraham, other Gentiles could be declared as righteous without being circumcised because they, too, could rely on faith, or trust in God's fidelity rather than on doing "the works of the Law," in this case circumcision, to be in right relationship with God.

Paul had not established the church at Rome, but he did intend to visit it on his way to Spain (Rom 15:24, 28). In the opening chapters of the letter, he is evenhanded in what he says about Jews and Gentiles. Neither has an advantage over the other when it comes to God's grace and salvation (Rom 1:16; 2:12; 3:23–24), both are under the power of sin (Rom 3:9–18), and God is the God of both (Rom 3:29–30). In Romans 9:4–5 Paul lists the gifts that God has given to Israel:

> They are Israelites, and to them belong the adoption, the glory, the covenants, the giving of the law, the worship, and the promises; to them belong the patriarchs, and from them, according to the flesh, comes the Messiah, who is over all, God blessed forever. Amen.

In Romans 11:29, he affirms that those gifts and God's election of Israel are irrevocable. In 11:1, he states clearly that God has not rejected Israel, and he then identifies himself as an Israelite. Now, it is true that in these texts Paul is talking about Messianic Jews like himself whom he saw as a remnant of Israel. Still, he has a hopeful vision for those Jews who have not joined that remnant. The metaphor he uses to describe the relationships of non-Messianic Jews, Messianic Jews, and Gentiles is the olive tree (Rom 11:17–24). Awkwardly, he speaks of some branches being cut off (non-Messianic

Jews) to make room for wild olive shoots (Gentiles) to be grafted onto the root of the olive tree (Messianic Jews). But he is quick to warn the Gentiles not to boast of the place they have been given on the root, because the natural branches (non-Messianic Jews) could easily be regrafted onto the root to replace the wild olive shoots (Gentiles). Ultimately, he concludes that "all Israel will be saved" (Rom 11:26).

Matthew Thiessen has sharpened the focus on these issues in Galatians and Romans. Along with a growing number of New Testament scholars, Thiessen in *A Jewish Paul* places Paul squarely within Judaism. First, Thiessen reminds us that, contrary to many different interpretations of these two letters in the Pauline *corpus*, we must never lose sight of the fact that Paul is addressing Gentiles in both. Hence the subtitle of Thiessen's book: *The Messiah's Herald to the Gentiles*. We know this from Romans itself, where Paul identifies himself as "God's envoy" (1:1 and 11:13). He makes the same claim in Galatians 1:15–16 and 2:7–8. The notion of Paul as God's "envoy to the Gentiles" even became part of the post-Pauline tradition (Acts 14:27; 15:12, 23; 21:19; 22:21; Eph 3:1–8, Col 1:24–27).[2]

To make sense of these many instances where Paul stresses his role as God's "envoy to the Gentiles," Thiessen stresses the heart of the challenge the Gentiles presented to Paul—namely, how to introduce them to the Jewish Messiah that Paul preached. Whereas many commentators on Romans understand Paul to be addressing the depravity of humans in general, Thiessen reads him, especially in 1:18–32, to be addressing only Gentiles. From this, the Gentile problem unfolds: They have a limited knowledge of God, which they get from observing the created world; they do not have what they could know about God from the Jewish Scriptures; as a result, they cannot honor God or give thanks to God, and they make foolish choices leading to the practice of idolatry. How will preaching the Messiah to them solve the Gentile problem?[3]

As already noted above, one aspect of Paul's solution to the Gentile problem was to include them in the promise God made to Abraham (Gen 12:1–3). The last part of that promise stated that "in [Abraham] all the families of the earth shall be blessed." When the Hebrew Bible was translated into Greek, the Hebrew word for families, *mishpechoth*, was translated with the Greek word for nations, *ta ethnē*, which in Paul's day also meant Gentiles. And so, Paul understood that the Gentiles, too, were heirs to the promise made to Abraham. Let us try to understand more fully how Paul saw Gentiles as Abraham's heirs.

Thiessen effectively exposes how Romans 2:28–29, where Paul stresses that true circumcision is a matter of the heart and not the flesh, has been misread in the long history of interpretation. Thiessen retranslates the text to show that Paul does not use the words *true* or *real*. Instead, he talks about the "visible Jew" who has "in-flesh circumcision" and the "hidden Jew" who has "a heart circumcised by the spirit." It is not a contrast between "true" and "false." It simply says that in-flesh circumcision alone is not enough to "merit God's praise"; one must also have the "circumcision of the heart." Thiessen backs up this argument with texts from Scripture such as Jeremiah 9:25–26, and he shows how Paul himself rejects the notion that he dismissed the importance of circumcision in Romans 3:2.[4] Regarding the Gentiles, then, Paul does not think circumcision is beneficial *to them*; it is a form of mutilation *for them* (Phil 3:2). He would not think the same about Jews. Thus, it is important to remember that Paul is talking specifically to Gentiles when he says circumcision does not carry a value *for them*.[5] Thiessen takes Paul at his word in 1 Corinthians 7:17–24 that everyone should remain in the state they were in when they were called to Jesus Messianism. Circumcised Jews should not seek to undo their circumcision, and Gentiles should not seek circumcision.[6]

Having established that Gentiles do not need to be circumcised because they are heirs of the promise made to Abraham concerning them, Thiessen goes one step further in establishing just how they are children of Abraham. In Galatians 3:29 Paul states, "And if you belong to Christ, then you are Abraham's offspring, heirs according to the promise." Opponents to Paul, Jesus Messianists in Galatia, told the Galatians that they had to be circumcised to become heirs of Abraham. Not so, says Paul, because if they belong to the Messiah, they *are* Abraham's heirs by receiving the spirit of the Messiah, and circumcision is not only unnecessary but also of no benefit to them. As Paul writes in Galatians 3:27, in their baptism they were clothed with Christ. Thiessen understands this to mean that they were "wrapped" in Christ or "immersed" in Christ. In Galatians 3:16, Paul established that Christ is Abraham's offspring. Therefore, when they are immersed in the spirit of Christ, the spirit of the Messiah, they are connected to Abraham by that spirit and not by circumcision. It all happens by means of faith that the Gentiles are Abraham's heirs.[7]

Long-reigning assumptions about Paul drawing a sharp dichotomy between Jews and Gentiles, therefore, do not stand up to scrutiny. If anything, recent scholarship like Thiessen's has shed new light on the relationship between Jews and Gentiles in Galatians and Romans.

THE GOSPEL OF MATTHEW

Some New Testament scholars claim to find a form of supersessionism in the Gospel of Matthew. As proof, they point to the tension between pro-Jewish and apparently anti-Jewish passages in his Gospel. At times, Jesus appears to be a Jewish teacher who is interested in showing the continuity of his thought with Jewish institutions of old. Yet he also appears to be critical of those institutions, especially when debating with scribes and Pharisees. Some interpret these texts as decidedly anti-Jewish. To resolve the tension in these two views, the late Daniel J. Harrington, SJ, in his commentary *The Gospel of Matthew* located the Gospel in the social and religious context of late Second Temple Judaism. Without suggesting that there was a monolithic form of Judaism when Matthew composed his Gospel, Harrington understands that Gospel as Matthew's response to a set of problems that all Jews at the time faced, having lost the institutions they had come to rely on, most notably the Jerusalem Temple, which was destroyed by the Romans in 70 CE. A brief examination of the historical context of that problem is needed before returning to the texts that are putatively pro-Jewish or anti-Jewish.

Harrington in his commentary identifies three different ways in which Jews responded to the destruction of the Jerusalem

Temple.[8] The first way he characterizes as an *apocalyptic response*. This was a response steeped in the Jewish apocalyptic tradition, which saw history divided into two phases: *a present age* marked by oppression or crisis among Jews trying to remain faithful to God, and a *future age* that would bring victory and vindication to the righteous. Examples of this response are found in the Book of Daniel in the Hebrew Bible and the Book of Revelation in the New Testament. Other examples, though not part of the biblical canon, would be 4 Ezra and 2 Baruch. Both books purportedly tell of the destruction of Jerusalem by the Babylonians in the sixth century BCE, even though (scholars concur) they were actually composed in the late first or early second century CE in response to the destruction of Jerusalem by the Romans in 70 CE. In the wake of this crisis of the Roman War, both books attempt to answer the question of how God could have allowed the fall of Jerusalem and the loss of the Temple to happen to the people of Israel.[9]

In 4 Ezra, that question is answered by delineating between two worlds that God had created: the *present world* and the *world to come* in which the wicked will be judged and punished and the righteous vindicated and rewarded. The Messiah will be revealed in the world to come and will establish a kingdom lasting four hundred years, after which he will die. The author of 4 Ezra exhorts those suffering in the present age to patient endurance, a common feature of apocalyptic literature, until the world to come is finally established. The Book of 2 Baruch shares some of the same features as 4 Ezra. History is viewed in two phases: the *present age* and the *age to come*. The present age is marked by tribulations that will be overcome in the age to come. Both books refer to the destruction of the Jerusalem Temple in 70 CE (4 Ezra 10:21; 2 Bar 32:3), the coming of a Messiah (4 Ezra 7:28; 2 Bar 39:7—40:2), and signs that accompany the arrival of the world/age to come (4 Ezra 4:52—5:13; 2 Bar 25:1–4). They differ, however, on the advice of how to conduct oneself in the present age until the arrival of the age to come. Whereas 4 Ezra counsels patient endurance (6:25–28; 7:17–18; 7:88–90) and adherence to the Torah, 2 Baruch advises that people only observe Torah (17:14; 44:2, 7; 48:24, 85:3).[10]

Harrington identifies the second response to the destruction of the Jerusalem Temple as the *rabbinic movement*.[11] Prior to 70 CE, three things were common to the variety of Judaisms in the first century CE: the Jerusalem Temple, the land of Israel, and the Torah. The various sectarian forms of Judaism agreed on the importance of these three factors, even if they did not always view them in the same way. The Essenes withdrew from Jerusalem to the shore of the Dead Sea over a disagreement with the Sadducees concerning their administration of the Temple. The Pharisees held a different understanding of the Torah from that of the Sadducees. Then, after 70 CE when the Temple had been destroyed and the land was occupied by the Romans, only the observance of Torah remained. In that context the rabbis emerged as a group of scholars who emphasized the study of the Torah and collected various interpretations of it. These interpretations were later codified in a series of rabbinic documents such as the Mishna, Tosefta, and Talmuds (Palestinian and Babylonian), Targums, and Midrashim.[12] According to Harrington, the traditions preserved in these documents are largely the work of two groups that are mentioned in the New Testament as the "scribes and the Pharisees." As a response to the fall of Jerusalem and the destruction of the Temple, the scribes and Pharisees shifted their focus to the study of the Torah, which was at the heart of rabbinic Judaism. The rabbinic movement emerged about one hundred years after the Gospel of Matthew was composed, but we can detect anticipations of that movement in the Gospel of Matthew.

Harrington identifies the third response to the fall of Jerusalem and the destruction of the Temple as *Jesus Messianism* as portrayed in the Gospel of Matthew.[13] Where the apocalyptic response of 4 Ezra and 2 Baruch focused on Torah as the guide to Jewish life in the present age in anticipation of the age to come, and the rabbinic response was to see in the Torah a way to be Jewish in the absence of the Temple and the land so that time and place became less important in how various forms of Judaism were observed, the Matthean Jesus Messianists had their own distinct interpretation of how to observe Torah, with the role of Jesus as an authoritative interpreter of it.[14]

The pro-Jewish texts of Matthew's Gospel confirm that Jesus's teaching on Torah was continuous with that of other Jewish groups in the first century CE. Jesus proclaims clearly that he has not come to destroy the Torah but to fulfill it (Matt 5:17).[15] He goes on to say that anyone breaking even the least of the commandments in Torah will be the least in the kingdom of heaven, and whoever keeps them and teaches them will be great in the kingdom of heaven. His overall conclusion about the value of Torah is that the righteousness of his listeners must exceed that of the scribes and Pharisees (Matt 5:19–20). By putting Jesus in this role, Matthew shows how the Jesus Messianists, for whom he wrote, compare with other Jewish groups who debated their own distinct interpretations of the Torah (14:27; 15:12, 23; 21:19; 22:21). For Matthew's community, Jesus concretizes his interpretation of Torah in the six antitheses found in the Sermon on the Mount (Matt 5:21—6:48). Harrington finds other pro-Jewish texts in Matthew's Gospel in the command to go to the lost sheep of the house of Israel (10:6 cf. 15:24) and in Jesus's counsel to the crowds and the disciples to follow the teachings of the scribes and Pharisees in a manner befitting Jesus Messianists (23:3).[16]

Matthew 23 needs to be seen against the background of criticisms leveled against the Jewish leadership that held authority in the wake of the destruction of Jerusalem in 70 CE. In *Matthew's Gospel and Formative Judaism*, J. Andrew Overman explores the sectarian antipathy toward local leaders, who some sectarian Jews felt had betrayed them and who were responsible for the hardships they were enduring.[17] He finds evidence of this criticism in 4 Ezra, 2 Baruch, 4 Baruch, the Psalms of Solomon, Lives of the Prophets, The Testament of Levi, and the Gospel of Matthew.

What about those passages that appear to be overtly anti-Jewish passages in Matthew's Gospel, particularly the woes he offers to the scribes and Pharisees, who are called hypocrites (23:15–36), and the self-curse uttered by the crowds in 27:25 ("His blood be on us and our children")? In "The Gradual Emergence of the Church and the Parting of the Ways," Harrington contextualizes these texts by showing their bivalent meaning as they refer simultaneously to the time of Jesus and to the later time of the

Matthean community.[18] Harrington understands the self-curse in Matthew 27:25 to span the time of Jesus and the time of the Matthean community. When the crowd says, "His blood be on us," the text refers the Jewish leadership in Jesus's day. When the text adds "and our children," it refers to the leadership in Matthew's day, since the curse can extend only to the next generation after Jesus. And so, it is not a curse against all Jews for all time.[19]

Harrington explains that these texts have at times been seen as antisemitic because they were read out of context, anachronistically. He argues that they need instead to be read within the context of the various crises that all Jews in the late first century CE experienced. As Harrington has shown, none of the three responses to the crises faced by all Jews after 70 CE constitute anti-Judaism or antisemitism. Matthew and his fellow Jesus Messianists still saw themselves as within Judaism. These responses illustrate the various ways late first-century CE Jewish groups underwent the process of identity and self-definition. That is not to deny that later Christian authors imputed anti-Judaism or antisemitism to Matthew's Gospel when they adopted supersessionist readings of Matthew. The attempt to replace Judaism with Christianity was an historical reality. Matthew, however, was not the originator of it. Reading his Gospel out of context is the real culprit.[20]

THE GOSPEL OF JOHN

John's Gospel has been viewed for some time as supersessionist for the way it portrays Jesus's interaction and confrontation with people in John's narrative simply identified as "the Jews." Focusing primarily on that term does not tell the whole story of the variety of Jews who appear in the Gospel. It is true that Jesus's dialogue with the Pharisees, also identified as "the Jews," in chapter 8 is at times harsh and strained when they confront him about who he claims to be and where he comes from (John 8:13–18). This stands in contrast to the group of Greek Jews in Jerusalem for the Passover who ask to see Jesus (12:20–26). And in 4:22, Jesus proclaims to a Samaritan woman that "salvation is from the Jews." How can we make sense of these different kinds of encounters?

Harrington convincingly shows how John and Matthew both saw themselves as authentic representatives of Judaism who continued the traditions of Judaism by portraying Jesus as an interpreter of the Jewish law (Matthew) or as the one who reveals the revelation of God (John). Harrington adds that Matthew's "instructor" and John's "Word of God" "probably looked to other Jews as going beyond the boundaries of Judaism." Finally, he points to another key feature that John's Gospel shares with Matthew's—namely, its bivalent temporality. It must be read on two levels: one at the time of Jesus, and the other at the time of the Johannine church.[21]

To get a fuller appreciation of the variety of ways in which John portrays Jews in his Gospel, we will first attend to this bilevel composition in order to see how it challenges the claim that John's gospel is supersessionist. Then we will look at other groups—"Jews (*Ioudaioi*)," "Galileans," and "Samaritans"—and how a proper understanding of these groups challenges a supersessionist reading of the Fourth Gospel.

The Diversity of Judaism in John's Gospel

Two important works that illustrate the bilevel composition of John's Gospel are John L. Martyn's *History and Theology in the Fourth Gospel*[22] and Raymond Brown's *The Community of the Beloved Disciple: The Life, Loves and Hates of an Individual Church in New Testament Times*.[23] While their respective approaches to understanding the origin and development of the Johannine community show nuanced differences, they both point in the same direction. First, the Gospel of John should be understood in view of the historical situation of the Johannine community. Second, John told the story of the Johannine church by telling the story of the story of Jesus.

The transparency of John's narrative for describing the situation of the Johannine community is perhaps best grasped in the story of Jesus healing a man who was blind from birth (John 9:1–41). On one level, the story tells of a confrontation between the Pharisees and Jesus over the healing, which took place on the Sabbath. On another level, it tells of the real fear that characters in the story have of the religious authorities who had the power to expel them from the synagogue. This is hinted at in the fact that the parents of the young man are reluctant to answer the Pharisees' question about him and how he was healed of his blindness. They tell the Pharisees to go ask the man himself because he is old enough to speak for himself. John explains their hesitancy with a parenthetical remark, "His parents said this because they were afraid of the Jews; for the Jews had already agreed that anyone who confessed Jesus to be the Messiah would be put out of the synagogue" (9:22). When the young man confesses to the Pharisees that Jesus must be from God because he was able to heal his blindness, the Pharisees respond by "driving him out," which means expulsion from the synagogue (9:34).

The threat reverberates elsewhere in the Gospel where others are described as being afraid of believing openly in Jesus. For instance, there is the figure of Nicodemus, who came to Jesus at night (3:2) presumably because he did not want to suffer the same fate as the man born blind. Nevertheless, because he is unable to commit to belief in Jesus, Nicodemus serves as an antitype of the young Judean man who had come to faith in Jesus after having been healed by him (9:38).

In chapter 12, John introduces a new group of Greek-speaking Jews who had come to Jerusalem to worship at Passover, and who asked Jesus's disciple Philip if they too could see Jesus. Philip relays the request to Jesus, who then describes the cost of discipleship illustrated by the grain of wheat which must die if it is to bear fruit (12:25). This sacrifice, demanded also of the followers of Jesus, serves as an encouragement for the Johannine community suffering social dislocation at the hands of the authorities in their local synagogue (see Matt 10:38; 16:24; Mark 8:34; Luke 14:27; 1 Cor 15:37). This is yet another example of how John's Gospel operates on two levels.

Jesus continues to speak about his impending death in the next scene, which is akin to the Gethsemane tradition found in the Synoptics (Matt 26:36–46; Mark 14:32–42; Luke 22:40–46). As soulful as this scene is, it does not meet with success among Jesus's listeners, for he leaves them and hides from them. John explains why. Despite the many signs he had worked among them, they did not believe in him. John captures the reasons why Jesus was not accepted by his own (see John 1:11) by citing Isaiah 6:9–10, a text that finds itself in similar explanations in other New Testament books (Matt 13:13–15; Mark 4:11–12; Luke 8:10; Acts 28:26–27; Rom 11:8, 10). Still John qualifies the explanation by claiming that many Jews, even some of the authorities, did believe in Jesus. They did not confess their belief openly because they feared the Pharisees and that they might be expelled from the synagogue. John's judgment concerning them is that they loved human glory more than the glory that comes from God (12:42–43).

These examples of people who want to follow Jesus and confess him openly, but who are intimidated by the Pharisees and fear of expulsion from the synagogue, tell the story of the Johannine church's struggle with the authorities of the synagogue to which they belonged. They are important clues to understanding the way John uses "the Jews" in a variety of contexts in his Gospel. As we have already seen, those identified as "the Jews" generally oppose Jesus (8:1–59), but some do believe in him (8:31; 12:20–26), although some of those do so only secretly (3:1–15; 19:38). Those Jews identified as coming from Galilee (Galileans), who were Jesus's closest followers, generally accept him (1:35–51; 3:26; 2:1–11). The Samaritans are like the Galileans in that they, too, receive Jesus (4:29–39). These varying portrayals suggest that John has grouped some Jews geographically and that their geographic origin relates to how they respond to Jesus.

Jouette Bassler, in "The Galileans: A Neglected Factor in Johannine Community Research," closely examines the Judeans and the Galileans in John and concludes that the geographical locations of Judea and Galilee are actually less important than the characterizations of people from those regions in their interaction with Jesus.[24] In general, Galileans accept Jesus because they can perceive his true identity (4:43–45). This can be said of some Judeans, like the man born blind, but not of others, like Nicodemus (3:1–21) and the Pharisees who debate with Jesus (8:1–59). And so, one can say that the Judeans generally represent individuals who do not understand Jesus's true identity and therefore reject him (5:1–18). The reason for that, however, is not because they are Jewish. Galileans, on the other hand, are receptive to Jesus because they know his identity (1:35–37; 6:14), recognize that he has been sent by God (6:33–34; 16:27–30; 9:33), and are thus able to believe in him.[25]

Although they are not as prominent as Galileans and Judeans in John, Samaritans are akin to Galileans insofar as they receive Jesus well—as a prophet (4:19) and possibly as the Messiah (4:29). Some Samaritans initially believe in Jesus on the word of the woman at the well (4:39), but many others believe in him based on his word that they themselves heard directly, so that they are convinced that he is the Savior of the world (4:42). It is not because they have come from Samaria but because of their own personal interaction with Jesus that they are able to perceive his true identity.[26]

Bassler tackles an anomaly in John's Gospel that could potentially undermine her argument. In 6:1, we learn that Jesus has returned to Galilee: "After this Jesus went to the other side of the Sea of Galilee, also called the Sea of Tiberias." There follows the feeding of the multitude, which the crowd receives enthusiastically (6:14), so much so that they want to make him a king (6:15). Jesus's response is to withdraw, which is not his usual response to acceptance by Galileans; rather, it typifies his response to rejection by Judeans (4:3; 5:13; 8:59; 10:40; 11:54). On the day after the feeding of the multitude, the crowd goes looking for Jesus and they travel to Capernaum where he was (6:25). Although this is happening in Galilee, Jesus's response to them is not as positive as the reader would have expected. He tells them they only came looking for him not because they saw signs, but because they had eaten the bread that he had given them. Elsewhere in the Gospel, people come to faith in Jesus when they see the signs (Johannine miracles) that he works. Signs faith in John is not full faith, but it may lead to full faith. In other words, this crowd that wanted to make him king has misunderstood who Jesus really is and therefore could not even exhibit the lowest form of faith in John's Gospel, signs faith. In 6:30 they ask a typically Judean question about what sign he will give them so that they might believe in him (2:18). He responds that he had given the sign of bread from heaven in the feeding of the multitude, an allusion to Moses and the manna in the wilderness (Exod 16:1–21). The questioners respond positively, "Sir, give us this bread always" (6:34), echoing the response of the Samaritan woman at the well: "Sir, give me this water, so that I may never be thirsty or have to keep coming here to draw water" (4:51).

In 6:41 the "Jews" (Judeans) reappear in the narrative, and they give the typical Judean response by complaining about Jesus because he claimed to be the bread that has come down from heaven. They continue to complain in 6:52, doubting that Jesus can give believers his flesh to eat. They are in Galilean territory, yet they render a response that would be at home in Judea. John thereby alerts the reader to the fact that he is more interested in the interaction of Galileans and Judeans with Jesus than in the geographic regions where they come from. Judeans can have a negative response to Jesus even if they are in Galilee, the region of positive responses to Jesus. Something else must be going on here. Presumably, Galileans can have a positive response to Jesus if they are in Judea (7:3; 11:7). The geographic terms have lost their spatial character and have taken on a symbolic one. Bassler explains that switch so: "Galileans symbolize those who receive the Word, Judeans symbolize those who reject it."[27]

There is more to it than a simple switch. Bassler has also shown that the terms *Ioudaioi* and *Galileans* mean different things in the Gospel's different layers. She actually refines Brown's and Martyn's views on the stages of the Johannine community's development as reflected in the Gospel. In the first stage of the community's formation, which is reflected in the first two chapters of the Gospel, "Galilean" means "a follower of Jesus." At a later stage, "Galileans" means "those who responded favorably to the Johannine message." Still later, when a "christological dispute" arises in the Johannine community, some members who could have been "Galileans" oppose Jesus and become like "Judeans." The final stage of the community's development involves the members' expulsion from the synagogue. That is when, according to Bassler, "Galileans" got its last connotation. Following Martyn's suggestion "that as it was impossible for Jesus to remain in Judea (e.g. 4:1–3)," she maintains that some of the members of the Johannine community realized "that it was impossible for them to remain in the synagogue."[28]

Bassler makes clear how the synagogue figures prominently in the way Judeans and Galileans express their faith in Jesus. As we have seen, Judeans such as Nicodemus (3:1–2), the parents of the man born blind (9:10–23), and Joseph of Arimathea (19:38) all fear that the authorities will expel them from the synagogue if they profess their faith in Jesus. The man born blind does not share this fear and comes to faith in Jesus freely (9:35–38). If one reads John's Gospel on two levels, then they should also understand the synagogue that way, since in John's day there would have been Judeans and Galileans in the synagogue. The symbolic value of that diversity speaks to the tension that must have existed in the synagogue, with the Galileans representing those who looked positively on the figure of Jesus and the Judeans representing those who held the opposite view and took issue with the Galilean perspective. If the first two chapters of the Gospel tell of the origin of the Johannine community in Galilee, then the rest of the Gospel speaks to the evolution of that community and the conflict over the true identity of Jesus among the Jewish groups featured in the Gospel, tempered by possible expulsion from the synagogue.[29]

Therefore, reading John's Gospel on two levels avoids reading it as supersessionist because it is a story of Jews who, like the Johannine community, know who Jesus is and accept what he reveals. The polemic in John's Gospel does not intend to replace Judaism with Christianity. Its purpose is to show the plurality of Jewish and Samaritan responses to Jesus within the context of the varieties of Judaism that existed in the first century.

Elsewhere in the Gospel we find additional stories of his relationship with the *Ioudaioi*, which is usually and problematically translated as "the Jews," as well as with Samaritans and Galileans. These relationships must be explored to get a fuller picture of whether a supersessionist reading of John's Gospel is viable.

The *Ioudaioi*

In addition to the five occurrences of *Ioudaioi* in chapter 8, usually translated as "the Jews," there are sixty-six occurrences in the singular or the plural throughout the rest of John's Gospel, not always with the same meaning. Paul Anderson in *The Riddle of the Fourth Gospel* has catalogued the various ways *Ioudaioi* is used in John.[30] Six times it refers simply to those people from the geographical region of Judea (4:3, 47, 54; 7:1, 3; 11:7). There are plenty of other references to "the Jews" opposing Jesus (5:16, 18; 7:1, 11, 13; 10:31, 33; 11:8; 18:31, 36, 38; 19:7, 12, 14, 38; 20:19). In yet other texts, they complain about Jesus, or they confront and challenge him and are divided over him, not understanding things he says and does (6:41, 52; 7:35; 8:22; 10:19, 24). Then there are places in John where "the Jews" are favorable toward Jesus (7:15, 31; 8:31; 10:42; 11:36). Sometimes "the Jews" are portrayed as sympathetic to Martha, Mary, and Jesus after the death of their brother, Lazarus (11:19, 31, 33). Some of those who witnessed the raising of Lazarus come to believe in Jesus while others go to the Pharisees to report what Jesus had done (11:45–46). In response, the Pharisees devise a plot to have Jesus killed, which prompts him to leave Judea and go north to Ephraim, because he did not feel safe in the south (11:54). But when Jesus returns to Bethany to visit Martha and Mary, many Jews came not on account of Jesus alone but also to see Lazarus, now raised from the dead (12:9), a cause for many more Jews to believe in Jesus (12:11). After that scene, Jews welcome him into Jerusalem, and those who had witnessed the raising of Lazarus continued to testify about Jesus (12:17). In other instances, "the Jews" are cast as leaders like Nicodemus (3:1) and Caiaphas (18:14) or as unnamed authorities (7:26, 48; 12:42), creating further ambiguity in the portrayal of "the Jews" in the Fourth Gospel. In short, the term *Ioudaioi* is used to designate a variety of people, some positively and some negatively, not just one monolithic group.[31]

The Galileans

Another distinct group of Jews are those who hail from Galilee, the northern part of Palestine from which Jesus himself had come. Hence, they are called the Galileans. Even though the term appears only once in John (4:45), there are many references to Galilee (1:43; 2:1, 11; 6:1; 7:1, 9, 41, 52; 12:21; 21:2) and Jesus's movement between it and Judea (4:3, 43, 47, 54). As we have already seen, the people of Galilee are receptive to Jesus and his message

(2:11; 4:45, 46). And so, the Galilean Jews offer a distinctly positive view of Jesus as they seem to know his true identity.

The Samaritans

Samaritans are mentioned only twice, once already seen in 8:48 where "the Jews" accuse Jesus of being a Samaritan, and earlier in a more positive light in 4:1–42, where Jesus engages in dialogue with a Samaritan woman. Their origins are not precisely known, but they derived their provenance from the northern region of Samaria, which was the capital of the kingdom of Israel. After the Assyrians took over the Northern Kingdom of Israel in 722 BCE, they exiled parts of the Israelite population and replaced them with other peoples. These new inhabitants intermarried with Israelites, and it is thought that the Samaritans could have originated from the resultant populations. Samaritans disagreed with the Jewish understanding of Scripture and adopted their own version of the Pentateuch. Their main place of worship was a sacred mountain, Mt. Gerizim (John 4:20), and not Jerusalem, where Jews worshipped. They even had a different notion of the Messiah, whom they called the *Taheb*. The New Testament highlights tensions between Jews and Samaritans (John 4:9; 8:48), which were often exacerbated by the fact that Jews had to travel through Samaritan territory to get to Jerusalem (Luke 17:11). Still, they saw themselves as Israelites. They may have interacted with Judean Jews, but generally their contact was restricted, as reflected in the parenthetical note in John 4:9, "Jews do not share things in common with Samaritans."

The Samaritan woman asks Jesus a question, "Are you greater than our father Jacob?" (4:12), not unlike the one about Abraham asked by the *Ioudaioi* in 8:53. In contrast to them, the Samaritan woman accepts Jesus as the Messiah (4:29). Moreover, the local Samaritans believe in Jesus because of the woman's testimony about him (4:39) and even ask him to stay with them. John tells his readers that many Samaritans believed in him because of Jesus's word, not hers, and they confess to the woman, "It is no longer because of what you said that we believe, for we have heard for ourselves, and we know that this is truly the Savior of the world" (4:39–42). Their positive response echoes that of the Galileans.

John's portrayal of these three Jewish groups—"the Jews," "Galileans," and "Samaritans"—argues against a supersessionist intent on John's part. John uses these various Jewish and Samaritan constituencies to encourage members of his community to discern what their response to Jesus will be, and he does this from within Judaism. He is not promoting Christianity as a replacement for Judaism. He is simply describing a variety of stances toward Jesus that his readers have experienced in their own lives to help them decide on where they stand in relation to Jesus.

HEBREWS

In ecclesial documents, preaching, and academic studies, the Epistle to the Hebrews has long been assumed to be supersessionist. One example from the document of the Council of Trent (1545–1563), "The Teaching and Canons of the Most Holy Sacrifice of the Mass," is instructive:

> As there was no fulfillment under the old covenant because of the powerlessness of the Levitical priesthood (as the apostle Paul testifies), it was necessary (God the Father of mercies thus ordaining) for another priest to arise according to the order of Melchisedech, our lord Jesus Christ, who was able to bring to completion all due to be sanctified and to lead them to perfection. And so, he our Lord and God, was to offer himself once to God the Father on the altar of the cross, a death thereby occurring that would secure for them eternal redemption.[32]

At the outset of this statement, the council denigrated the Jewish Law by claiming that the Levitical priesthood was ineffective, having been replaced by the high priesthood of Christ as supposedly espoused in Hebrews. The idea that Christ's "once for all" sacrifice was superior to repetitive sacrifices of the Jewish Law has persisted in the interpretation of Hebrews to the present day.[33] Philip Church in "Hebrews and the Question of Supersessionism" tries to maintain a middle view that, in Hebrews, it is not Israel that is replaced but its "religious system that is superseded."[34] This distinction, however, is unhelpful because it is difficult to separate the covenant, the temple, sacrifices, and Israel's scriptures from Judaism itself, as if they constituted a separate "religious system."

What drives the supersessionist interpretation of Hebrews is the author's use of rhetorical *synkrisis* (comparison) of the Levitical cult with the Jesus Messianists' understanding of their rituals. The use of the word *better* in texts discussing the sanctuary, the priesthood, the covenant, and sacrifice would seem to suggest the *replacement* of these Jewish institutions with better forms of them that have been brought about by the coming of Jesus Christ.[35] Understanding the genre, purpose, and circumstances of Hebrews will show that supersessionist reading of it is incorrect. Ostensibly, Hebrews takes the form of a letter with typical epistolographic features, but it is actually a homily preached for a community that was flagging in faith. To that end, the author describes his homily as "a word of exhortation" or a "word of encouragement" (Heb 13:22). Composed after the destruction of Jerusalem in 70 CE, which brought about the loss of the Temple, the cessations of sacrifice, and changes to the Levitical priesthood, the purpose of Hebrews is to console and encourage its recipients by stressing continuity with their Jewish past.[36] It does not oppose Judaism to Christianity, but rather intends to shore up the faith of the community for which it was composed. There is no identifiable form of first-century CE Judaism that has been replaced by Christ described in the homily. The author does not dwell on what the recipients have lost of their Jewish heritage; he addresses instead what this community still had of that heritage. The catalogue of their spiritual possessions is impressive: hope (6:19), a great High Priest (4:14–15; 8:1; 10:21), and confidence (3:14; 10:19, 35; 13:6). They do lack a lasting city on earth (13:14), but they have hope in an eschatological future, where they will enter into God's rest (4:1, 9–11) in a heavenly Jerusalem (12:22) and will receive a kingdom that cannot be shaken (12:28).[37] The author stresses, too, that they still have a heavenly sanctuary (9:24; 10:19), an altar (13:10), and a spiritualized sacrifice of praise (13:15).[38] Moreover, the author reminds his listeners that the covenant has not been abrogated.

Indeed, they have a new covenant that is continuous with the old one (8:8, 13; 9:15; 12:24).[39]

Hence, as with the other New Testament books surveyed here, Hebrews, when read as having been written for Jewish Messianists who saw themselves as living within Judaism, cannot properly be understood as a form of incipient supersessionism. Viewing the author's purpose to offer consolation to his audience redirects Hebrews away from a supersessionist interpretation. To understand Hebrews in this way is to place it within Judaism and not against it.

In "The Relationship of the Old and the New Covenant as One of the Central Issues in Jewish-Christian Dialogue," Cardinal Walter Kasper clearly states that Hebrews should not be read from a supersessionist perspective and that such a reading creates an obstacle to progress in Jewish-Christian dialogue:

> It is this context which must be understood when the Epistle sets up the contrast between the first purely earthly covenant and a second better (cf. *Heb 8:7*) and new covenant (cf. *9:15, 12:24*). The first covenant is defined as outdated, in decline and doomed to obsolescence (cf. *8:13*), while the second covenant is defined as everlasting (cf. *13:20*). To establish the foundations of this contrast the Epistle refers to the promise of a new covenant in *Jer 31:31–34* (cf. *Heb 8:8–12*). This demonstrates that the Epistle to the Hebrews has no intention of proving the promises of the old covenant to be false, but on the contrary treats them as valid. The reference to the Old Testament promises is intended to help Christians to be sure of their salvation in Christ. At issue in the Epistle to the Hebrews is not the contrast of the old and new covenants as we understand them today, nor a contrast between the church and Judaism, but a contrast between the eternal heavenly priesthood of Christ and the transitory earthly Levitical priesthood. (§3)[40]

CONCLUSION

This chapter has engaged the question of whether New Testament books that have been interpreted as supersessionist actually promote a replacement theology. I have argued that the first-century situation of the composition of the New Testament was much more fluid and certainly more complex than any simple charge of supersessionism would permit. The work of Thiessen on Galatians and Romans places Paul and his letters squarely within Judaism, even while Paul is writing to Gentiles. Daniel Harrington's view of the problematic texts in Matthew's Gospel shows that they do not lend themselves to supersessionist interpretation because they straddle two time periods, the time of Jesus (4 BCE–33 CE) and the time of the Matthean community. His bivalent interpretation locates the putative anti-Jewish texts of Matthew within the debate with synagogue authorities (post 70 CE). He has also shown that Matthew's Gospel was written as a response to the destruction of Jerusalem and the Temple that existed alongside the apocalyptic response made by other Jews in Matthew's day as well as the response of later rabbinic Judaism. The same is true with the Gospel of John in the late first century CE: there was no replacement theology in the debates over the identity of Jesus and the formation of the Johannine community. Rather, there are a variety of responses to Jesus that characterize a corresponding variety of Jews in the Gospel—*Ioudaioi*, Judeans, Galileans, and Samaritans. When John's Gospel is read not only as the story of Jesus but also as the story of the formation and evolution of the Johannine community, the supposed supersessionism of the Gospel dissolves into a quest for the identity and self-definition of the latter seen in relation to the identity of Jesus. It, too, remains within Judaism. Finally, the consoling homily of Hebrews is intended to encourage and support a community that fears that with the destruction of the Jerusalem Temple it has lost its Jewish heritage. It aims at showing the continuity of the community for which it was written with the legacy of their Judaism. It is addressed to followers of Jesus who understand themselves still to be a part of Judaism.

To speak of distinct entities known as Christianity and Judaism in the first century CE would be premature. In the first century CE, the notion of "religion" was not established in a way that can easily be applied to groups of individuals devoted to particular gods and engaged in rituals that today we might identify as religious. Moreover, Jesus's followers did not identify as Christians; they saw themselves as Jews. The Greek term *Christianos* should be translated "Messianists," meaning "followers of the anointed one," the Messiah (Acts 11:26). As we have seen, Judaism was not a monolithic entity. Within the New Testament itself different sects of Judaism are identified—Pharisees, Sadducees, Zealots, Herodians, Essenes, and Messianic Jews like the followers of Jesus. There were also Jews that do not fall easily within any of those group designations, such as the *'am ha'aretz*, "the people of the land," about whom very little is known. Whereas in the past some scholars have pointed to an incipient supersessionism in the letters of Paul, particularly in Romans and Galatians, or the Gospels of Matthew and John and in the homily that is Hebrews, such positions no longer seem tenable when these New Testament books are read within the broader context of first-century Judaism and not apart from it.

In the next chapter we will examine the beginnings of supersessionism in second-century CE Christian authors in their efforts to distinguish Christianity from Greek and Roman cults and Judaism. Their goal to portray Christianity as superior to those other forms of devotion, sacrifice, and worship will inevitably place other religions in an inferior position and, regarding Judaism, will advocate for its replacement with Christianity.

Chapter Three

THE ADVENT OF CHRISTIAN SUPERSESSIONISM IN THE SECOND CENTURY AND ITS LATER GROWTH

Having argued in the previous chapter that New Testament texts are not supersessionist, I turn now to tracing the beginnings of supersessionist biblical interpretation among Christian writers in the second century CE. In chapter 1, we already examined the *Epistle of Barnabas*, a second-century text purported to have been written by the coworker of Paul; it was circulated but never made it into the scriptural canon, although it is found in one New Testament manuscript, the Codex Sinaiticus. Now we will shift focus to Christian thinkers writing for a broader audience as they made a case for the intellectual and moral legitimacy of Christianity; most of the texts we will consider became authoritative for later generations of Christian thinkers. While it is difficult to understand the motivation of these authors for speaking against Judaism in service of the elevation of Christianity and even its replacement, the reality of supersessionist theology from the second century on must be addressed openly and honestly if the mistakes of the past are not to be repeated in the present and future. Because the fourth century was an especially problematic one for the dissemination of supersessionism, I will look at what John Chrysostom (347–407

CE) preached against Judaizing Christians in Syrian Antioch. This chapter will close with a brief examination of the *Adversos Judeos* (*Against the Jews*) traditions that grew out of the anti-Jewish polemics of the fourth century. My overall purpose in this chapter is to show that, unlike the first century CE when Jews and Christians debated about their likenesses and differences, from the second century CE and later those debates became external to Judaism as Christianity more and more asserted itself over and against Judaism, giving birth to an antagonistic supersessionism.

Among the first authors to introduce supersessionism in Christian biblical interpretation are those who are referred to as "apologists." These authors undertook the defense (*apologia*) of Christianity primarily against Greek and Roman religions in order to prove that Christianity was not inferior to them in its philosophy, theology, and rituals. Due to the close association of Christianity and Judaism in the minds of Greeks and Romans, it seemed necessary for Christian apologists to distinguish Christianity from Judaism so as to counter Greek and Roman criticisms that Christianity's inferiority as a religion could not be divorced from its origins in Judaism. This led inevitably to anti-Judaism and supersessionism in Christian thought from the second century CE on. That history is a long and complex one. In this chapter, I offer some examples of early supersessionist texts and the basic theological and exegetical principles they established. These principles would remain fairly stable over subsequent centuries, even as contexts changed and attitudes intensified. The examples of supersessionist thought in this chapter are therefore meant to be illustrative, not exhaustive.

THE EPISTLE TO DIOGNETUS

One of the first apologies written, *The Epistle to Diognetus*, was most likely composed between 70 and 135 CE, with some scholars preferring a more precise date around 130.[1] This anonymous writing of the second century is putatively written by Mathetes, whose name means "disciple" in Greek, to Diognetus. The name is common for the time, and so the exact identity of the recipient is not known. The letter's purpose is to show the superiority of Christianity over Greek idolatry primarily and Jewish worship secondarily. The latter is not referred to as a religion but is rather called a superstition (*Diognetus*, 1.1), ancient Roman shorthand for cults that frequently originated in the Eastern part of the Roman Empire (Acts 26:26; Tacitus, *Annals* 15.44). The irony, of course, is that imperial Rome denied Christianity the status of a legitimate religion (*religio licita*) that it had given to Judaism, and it was Christianity that was considered a superstition.

Holding a strict separation between Jews and Christians, the author makes clear that Christians do not worship as Jews do. Some scholars see the simple question of how Christians differ from Jews in their worship of God as the heart of this section of the third chapter of the letter, but there appears to be more to it than that in Mathetes's attempt to answer the question. Standard translations of the letter show Mathetes addressing Diognetus's desire to know why Christians do not worship as do Jews (*Diognetus*, 3.1). A more accurate translation has Mathetes addressing Diognetus's anxiety over the issue. Why anxiety? Is it because of the closeness of Christianity to Judaism that Mathetes wants to distinguish so sharply between the worship practices of the two religions to avoid confusing Christians and Jews for his Greek readers? Or is it to make clear for his Christian readers why they no longer follow Jewish ritual practices? It seems that Diognetus is interested in more than mere descriptions of the forms of worship in these two religions. According to Jefford, his goal is to show that Jews worship God the way Greeks do.[2]

For that reason, Mathetes begins with a comparison of Jewish worship to that of Greek religions. His first point is to compare the nature of the gods worshipped by Greeks and Jews (2.1–10). For the Greeks, those whom they call gods are material objects rather than living gods. They are made of stone, wood, silver, iron, or pottery. They are all perishable and insensate: deaf, blind, lifeless, and motionless (*Diognetus*, 2.4). This description of Greek gods as idols hearkens to the idol parodies of the Hebrew prophets (Isa 40:18–19; 44:9–20; 46:5–8; Jer 10:1–16). Jews therefore have an advantage over Greeks because they shun idol worship (3.2) in favor of worshipping God as the absolute ruler of the universe.

The nature of God in Jewish worship is not the issue for Mathetes. Curiously, in this same section of the letter he likens Jewish worship to that of Greeks. His purpose is to show that Christian worship is superior to both Greek and Jewish worship. Greeks worship gods as though those gods needed their worship. Jews get it right in proclaiming the nature of their God as the absolute ruler of the universe. To that extent they are no different from Christians, who worship a completely self-sufficient God. Why, then, is it necessary for Mathetes to shift his attention away from the Jews' correct notion of the nature of God to focus on their ritual practices? He does it to show how those practices are actually like Greek idolatry because both involve blood, smoke, and burnt offerings. He suggests that, like the Greek gods, the Jewish God requires those rituals and that the Jewish God must not be self-sufficient. This is an insult to Jewish worship, but it accomplishes Mathetes's goal of separating Christians from Jews in the matter of how they worship. This move pivots away from the fact that Jews worship a God worthy of their worship to the charge that Jewish rituals are not different from Greek idolatry. Of those rituals, Mathetes writes:

> Yet those who sacrifice to him with blood and fat and whole burnt offerings and honor him with these offerings seems to me no different than those who show the same copious honor to deaf images. One people makes offerings to those who cannot receive the honor; the others believe that they are giving to one who needs nothing. (*Diognetus*, 3.5)

The fourth chapter of the letter explains why Mathetes can equate Jewish ritual with Greek idolatry. In perhaps the harshest section of the letter, he excoriates Jewish dietary laws, Sabbath observance, circumcision, observance of festivals and new moons as absurdities (*Diognetus*, 4.1). He poses a series of searing questions:

> For how is it not illegitimate to accept some things that God made for human use as created good and to reject

> others as worthless and unnecessary? And how is it not immoral to malign God by saying that he forbids that anything good be done on the sabbath? And how is it not absurd to boast in the mutilation of the flesh as evidence of election, as if on this basis they were especially loved by God? And their stargazing and moon watching to determine months and days, and how they differentiate within God's organized world and among changes of seasons as they are inclined, choosing some for feasts and some for mourning—who would consider this proof of their reverence rather than imprudence? So I suppose that you have learned enough about how Christians do well to keep away from the general silliness and deceit, officiousness and arrogance of Jews. (*Diognetus*, 4.2–6)

The reduction of Jewish ritual practices to the equivalent of Greek idolatry is peculiar at this point in the letter. The bulk of the letter deals with the superiority of Christianity over Greek religion. It would have been sufficient for Mathetes simply to continue his argument along those lines. Nonetheless, after showing the initial shortcomings of Greek worship in chapter 2, he turns to his comparison of Christianity and Judaism. Oddly, Mathetes's criticisms of Jewish worship do not reflect any known form of Judaism in the mid-second century CE. What he claims about the observance of the Sabbath and festival days, new moons, and circumcision is a caricature of Jewish ritual customs designed to elevate Christian worship and praise it for replacing those rituals with its own. His reduction of Jewish ritual customs to the equivalent of Greek idolatry is purely gratuitous. In stark contrast, he praises Christianity for abstaining from the vanity of Jewish worship, labeled as some form of officiousness and arrogance. Likewise, Christianity merits praise for avoiding the empty worship of Greek religion.

Describing Judaism or any of its customs or practices as inferior to Christianity is a stock element of supersessionism. And so, it is not surprising that an assault on Jewish worship finds itself in a letter whose purpose is to set forth the distinctiveness and excellence of Christianity over other religions of the day.

JUSTIN MARTYR

Justin Martyr was a native of Samaria in Northern Palestine, born in the Roman colony of Flavia Neapolis. Some scholars identify him as a Samaritan or as someone from a region populated by Palestinians and Samaritans. As we saw in chapter 2, the latter were a semitic people akin to Jews, but whom Jews did not accept as authentically Jewish. Justin was a philosopher who converted to Christianity, started a school of Christian philosophy in Rome, and was ultimately martyred during the reign of Marcus Aurelius sometime between 162 and 168 CE for refusing to sacrifice to the Roman gods. With respect to Jews and supersessionism, two of Justin's writings are source texts: the *First Apology* and *The Dialogue with Trypho*.

Justin's *First Apology*

Justin addressed his *First Apology* to the Roman Emperor Antoninus Pius and two of his adopted sons: Verissimus, better known as Marcus Aurelius, and Lucius, also known as Lucius Verus.[3] The object of the apology is the defense of Christianity against the charge of atheism, meaning impiety toward the Roman gods. Even so, it contains a fair amount of comparison between Christianity and Judaism.

There are multiple references to Jews in the *First Apology*. Justin complains about how Jews misunderstand their own Scriptures, how they lack a proper knowledge of God, and how they inflicted punishment on Jesus Christ. A prominent theme for him is how it was possible for Israel to have known Christ through the utterances of its prophets. The supersessionist objective of this line of inquiry is designed to show that the things which were prophesied in Hebrew Scriptures were fulfilled in Jesus Christ. Justin argues that prior to his earthly life, Christ as the Word was active in Jewish prophecy, although not visible as Christ. The result is to render the Hebrew Bible as a mere preparation for the New Testament, a stock element of supersessionism.

Justin's interpretation of the story of Moses at the burning bush (Exod 3:1–6) serves as an example of this interpretive move.

He does not deny that God spoke to Moses, something that Jews in Justin's day acknowledged (*First Apology* 63.1). Yet he then cites Isaiah 1:3, "The ox knows its owner and the donkey its master's crib; but Israel does not know, my people do not understand," to claim that Jews did not understand the true meaning of what God had spoken to Moses. He likens the Isaiah citation to a version of a saying that occurs in Matthew 11:27 and Luke 10:22. Justin may have cited the saying from memory rather than from the written Gospels because it differs from their version of it: "No one knew the Father, except the Son or the Son except the Father and those to who the Son should reveal him" (*First Apology*, 63.3). Justin adds that the Jews did not know the Father or the Son, creating a proof for his charge that the Jews cannot understand their Scriptures because they lack a proper knowledge of God. Moreover, in drawing this comparison, Justin has found a way to insert Christ into the story of the burning bush, supposedly so as to explain how Jews fail to grasp the deeper meaning of their Scriptures. Consequently, they fail not only in their knowledge of God, but also in recognizing Christ. Not unlike the author of the *Epistle of Barnabas*, Justin follows a method of scriptural interpretation that depends on typology and allegory as it eschews the literal meaning of the text—and therefore also challenges what Jews might claim is the correct way to read Scripture.

In the story of the burning bush (Exod 3:1–15), Moses encounters an angel in the form of a flame of fire. Justin identifies that angel christologically. For Justin, Christ as Son is none other than the Logos, the preexistent Christ, who can take other visible forms. Even though the angel does not speak in the original story from Exodus, Justin has Christ, the Logos—an angel in the form of a flame—reveal God's personal name, "I am who is." He says as much when he concludes, "But those utterances were made as a demonstration that Jesus Christ is the Son of God and apostle and was formerly the Logos and was sometimes revealed in the form of fire and sometimes in an incorporeal image" (*First Apology*, 63.10). As Oskar Skarsaune has shown in *The Proof from Prophecy*, generally all of Justin's Old Testament theophanies (appearances of God) are also Christophanies (appearances of Christ).[4]

Justin introduces another problematic addition to the story: "But now, having become a human being by the will of God for the sake of the human race, he endured also to suffer what treatment the demons made him endure at the hands of the unthinking Jews" (*First Apology,* 63.10). This linking of the suffering and death of Jesus at the hands of the Jews to their misunderstanding of Hebrew Scriptures is repeated throughout the *First Apology* at 35.1–9; 36.1–3; 37.1—38.8; and 49.5.

Justin's entire interpretation of Hebrew Scripture is premised on his belief that the only true understanding of its prophecies is a Christian one. Pressing that point, he attempts to show that those prophecies have meaning only insofar as they are fulfilled in the New Testament. For this reason, he must interpret stories like that of the burning bush by using typology to show where Christ is hidden in the text. Such an approach denies that the Hebrew Bible has an integrity of its own as a single testament. The irony is, of course, that before there was a New Testament, Jesus Messianists and early Christians used the Greek translation of the Hebrew Bible as their Scripture, making them a one-testament people as well.

Justin's *Dialogue with Trypho*

The Dialogue with Trypho is a putative dialogue between Justin, a Christian philosopher, and Trypho, a diaspora Jew. Whereas the identity of Justin is known, determining the identity of Trypho is fraught with difficulty. At one time it was customary to equate him with Tarfon, a rabbi and priest who lived between 70 and 135 CE. This theory has fallen by the wayside, mainly because Trypho does not seem to be a representative of rabbinic Judaism like Tarfon.[5]

Some scholars think of Trypho as a fictitious dialogue partner created by Justin. Trypho may have been a foil for Justin to supply him with questions about Trypho's Judaism that Justin wanted to answer from his Christian and supersessionist perspective.[6] If true, readers will not get an accurate view of Judaism in Justin's day, even though they will glean Justin's perspective on contemporaneous Judaism. Also, if true, the *Dialogue* would not be a true dialogue because it only presents Justin's view of Judaism.[7] It is not uncommon for supersessionist views of Christianity to be based on inaccurate or anachronistic views of the form of Judaism that they critique.

Other scholars see Trypho as a real person engaged in a real dialogue with Justin. This is not a majority view among scholars, and it raises more questions about Trypho and his Judaism than it answers. What kind of Jew was Trypho? Some have identified him as a Pharisee, while others portray him as a rabbinic Jew, and still others call him a Hellenistic Jew. Where was he located? In the absence of identifying geographic markers in the *Dialogue* it is difficult to pin a location on Trypho. There are scholars who simply accept the view of the early fourth-century Church historian Eusebius of Caesarea in his *Ecclesiastical History* (4.18.6) that Justin wrote a *Dialogue against the Jews* in Ephesus placing Trypho and the *Dialogue* in that city.[8] But this is inconsistent with Trypho's self-identification in the *Dialogue* itself:

> Trypho, he said, is my name. I am a Hebrew of the circumcision, a refugee from the recent war, and at present a resident of Greece, mostly in Corinth.[9] (*Dialogue*, 1.1)

Still trusting in Eusebius, some scholars identify Trypho as a Jew from Asia Minor.

The extant text of the *Dialogue* presents its own problems. How should one understand the large sections of prophetic scriptural texts that take up a fair amount of space in the document? What form of Judaism is represented in the *Dialogue* itself? Has the text undergone revisions by Justin after an initial draft of it was complete? Within the context of the dialogue both Justin and Trypho engage with each other over their respective views of Judaism as well as Christianity and Greek religion. But are they just that? Is Justin putting words in Trypho's mouth for the sake of his larger apologetic purpose? At the very least, the *Dialogue*'s stated purpose is to offer a defense of Christianity against Greek religion, with some views on Judaism to help to make distinctions among these three religions.[10] Putting those scholarly concerns aside, our concern here is the relevance of this text as a witness to the advent of supersessionism in the second century CE.

In the *Dialogue*, Justin's interests in Judaism center on the Jewish law, circumcision, the Sabbath, the Messiah, and the penalty for the death of Jesus.

Jewish Law

One of the first issues raised by Trypho is the fact that Christians do not observe Jewish law and its prescribed practices. Justin poses a fundamental question to Trypho and his friends: whether the only accusation they have against Christians is that they do not observe the law, or circumcision, or the Sabbath. But he joins to those issues some of the common criticisms made against Christians by non-Jews. Those criticisms were not just about what Christians believed but also about how they behaved. They involved charges of serious immorality, such as cannibalism and wanton sexual behavior at Christian meals (*Dialogue* 10.1). Such false criticisms stemmed from prejudicial rumors about the consumption of the Eucharist as the body and blood of Christ; about the Christian love command observed in the context of fictive kinship where Christians were known as brothers and sisters; and about the sacrifice and consumption of infants during sexual rituals. Such accusations and prejudices were recounted by other ancient authors such as Epiphanius and Origen. Taking the high road, Trypho shows himself to be eminently reasonable and rejects these moral criticisms as being "too repulsive to human nature" (*Dialogue* 10.2). He further supports his avoidance of those rumored untoward practices with his reading of the Christian Gospels, which do not support such criticisms.

Such ignorance, however, does not absolve Christians from questions about their lifestyle because, in Trypho's opinion, there are other shortcomings that result from their not observing the Jewish law. More concerning to him is that Christians see themselves as different from other people—more particularly, as holier than others. Yet they do not segregate themselves from others, and they follow a lifestyle not that different from that of Gentiles, precisely because they do not keep the feasts or Sabbaths or practice the rite of circumcision. He is even more apprehensive of what Christians believe about Christ. He comments on their faith, "You place your hope in a crucified man, and still expect to receive favors from God when you disregard his commandments" (*Dialogue* 10.3). Trypho equates these Christian failures to scorning the covenant and spurning its commands. And so, he levels a charge of hypocrisy against Christians: "...you try to convince us that you know God, when you fail to do those things that every God-fearing person would do" (*Dialogue* 10.3).

In response, Justin proclaims a common belief in the same God for Christians and Jews, but he undermines that appeal to commonality when he tries to contextualize the Christian understanding of the Jewish law. He distinguishes between a universal law for all humans and the law given to Jews, but he sets them in opposition to one another, claiming that one abrogates the other. He writes,

> The law promulgated at Horeb is already obsolete, and was intended for you Jews only, whereas the law of which I speak is simply for all men. Now a later law in opposition to an older law abrogates the older; so too, does a later covenant void an earlier one. An everlasting and final law, Christ himself, and a trustworthy covenant has been given to us, after which there will be no law or commandment or precept. (*Dialogue* 11.2)

In effect, a metaphorical Christ has put an end to the Jewish law. This erroneous belief will become one of the standard tenets of supersessionism.

To shore up this idea of a replaced law and covenant he includes two proof texts, one from Isaiah 51:4–5 and the other from Jeremiah 31:31–32, both of which mention a law for the "nations" and a new covenant for Israel. Jews, of course, did not interpret those two prophetic texts to mean that a universal law was given to the "nations," meaning Gentiles, or that the new covenant of Jeremiah was a replacement of any previous covenants that God had made with Israel. Justin's faulty exegesis had dire consequences for Jews, because law and the covenant have both been replaced with Christ (*Dialogue* 11.4). Notably, the law that Justin claims is for all people does not apply to Jews, who he believes have a law unto themselves.

He seems not to be aware of this contradiction. He pushes even further in the last part of this chapter, where he proclaims, in addition to the replacement of the law and the covenant, the very replacement of Israel itself:

> We have been led to God through this crucified Christ, and we are the true spiritual Israel, and the descendants of Judah, Isaac, and Abraham, who, though uncircumcised, was approved and blessed by God because of his faith and was called the father of many nations. All this shall be proved as we proceed with our discussion. (*Dialogue* 11.5)

Thus is Israel dispossessed of its divine heritage and historical lineage. Like Paul, Justin makes a distinction between, on the one hand, God's reckoning Abraham as righteous in Genesis 15:6 and, on the other hand, the later divine command of circumcision in Genesis 17:11–14, a distinction that will disappear in *Dialogue* 23.4. If Christ is a universal law for all, why can there not be a law, covenant, or circumcision for Jews? It is because Christianity has become a new spiritual Israel and Christ has become a new law and covenant, and Justin has spiritualized circumcision.[11]

Later in the *Dialogue* (25:1–6), Justin invokes a catena of texts from Isaiah 63:15—64:12 to show that Jews will not be the heirs of Abraham, prompting Trypho to ask, "Do I understand you to say that none of us Jews will inherit anything on the holy mountain of God?" (25.6). Justin responds, "I didn't say that, but I do say that those who have persecuted Christ in the past and still do, and do not repent, shall not inherit anything on the holy mountain, unless they repent" (*Dialogue* 26.1). In *Dialogue* 28.2, Justin's idea of repentance includes conversion to Christianity. Trypho retorts, not incorrectly, that Justin only quotes Scripture that he thinks agrees with his faulty claims but omits texts that show God's command to Israel to observe the Sabbath law, such as Isaiah 58:13–14. Justin's answer is hostile and offensive:

> I have not omitted such passages on purpose from the Prophets because they do not coincide with my teach-

> ing, but because (as you well understand), although God through his prophets gives you identical commands as he did through Moses, this was done only on account of your hardness of heart and ingratitude toward him. He repeated those precepts in the hope that even so you might possibly repent some time and thus please him, and no longer sacrifice your children to the demons, nor remain the *companions of thieves, nor lovers of gifts, nor seekers of rewards; judging not for the fatherless, nor suffering the cause of the widow to come unto you, nor having your hands full of blood* [Isa 1:23, 15]....Thus, as your sinfulness was the reason why God first issued those precepts, so now because of your enslavement to sin, or rather your greater inclination to it, by means of the same precepts, he calls you to remember and know him. But you are a ruthless, stupid, blind, and lame people, children in whom there is no faith. As God himself says, *Honoring him only with your lips, but your hearts are far from him, teaching your own doctrines* and not his [Isa 29:13]. (*Dialogue* 27.2–4)

The theme of the Jewish law as a punishment for the sins of Israel continues in *Dialogue* 19.6 and 67.8–10.

Circumcision

Just as Justin proclaimed that the Jewish law was obsolete, intended for Jews only, he says the same thing about circumcision. That obsolescence is the reason why he tells Trypho that Christians have no need of circumcision. Even more, he suggests that Jews should adopt the spiritual circumcision of Christianity:

> You Jews, who have the circumcision of the flesh, are in great need of our circumcision, whereas we, since we have our circumcision, do not need yours. For if, as you claim, circumcision had been necessary for salvation, God would not have created Adam as uncircumcised; nor would he have looked with favor upon the sacrifice

> of the uncircumcised Abel, nor would he have been pleased with the uncircumcised Enoch, who *was seen no more because God took him* [Gen 5:24]. (*Dialogue* 19.3)

Following this text, he lists two other ancient uncircumcised Israelites: Noah and Melchizedek. Even though in *Dialogue* 11.5 Justin listed Abraham among the uncircumcised, he acknowledges in this chapter that it was through Abraham that circumcision was introduced into Judaism (*Dialogue* 19.4). It is convenient for Justin to argue that Christians do not need Jewish circumcision because before Abraham there were Israelite ancestors who were not circumcised and were yet viewed as acceptable to God. But he undermines his argument by showing the necessity of circumcision from the time of Abraham. He disregards the history of Israel and the evolution of ritual practices to make an argument for the needless rite of circumcision for Christians, while acknowledging its necessity for Jews only.

Continuing with the explanation of why Christians do not observe the Jewish law, Justin finds yet another way to denigrate Judaism. He claims that circumcision was given to Israel as a punishment for its sins. After citing the Septuagint (Greek) version of Isaiah 1:16, "Wash yourselves, be clean, and take away evil from your souls," Justin offers this interpretation:

> Thus does God order you to be washed in this laver, and to be circumcised with the true circumcision. We, too, would observe your circumcision of the flesh, your Sabbath days, and, in a word, all your festivals, if we were not aware of the reason why they were imposed upon you, namely, because of your sins and your hardness of heart. (*Dialogue* 18.2)

In the following chapter he tries to lend further credence to this claim that the rite of circumcision is representative of the whole law. In another attempt to explain why Christians do not observe the Jewish law, Justin expands his answer to Trypho:

> As I already explained, I [Justin] answered, it is because circumcision is not for all men, but only for you Jews, to mark you off for the suffering you now so deservedly endure. Nor do we approve of your useless baptism of the wells, which has no connection at all with our baptism of life. Thus has God protested that you have forsaken him, *the fountain of living water, and have dug for yourselves broken cisterns which can hold no water.* (*Dialogue* 19.2)

Note how he identifies circumcision as another form of divine punishment. One reason for this view is that circumcision was so important to Judaism that it could be identified with the law. If the law was given as a punishment, then so also was circumcision. Instead of being an identity marker of the covenantal relationship with God, it becomes for Justin a way to identify who is a Jew, so that they may be persecuted. Furthermore, if the law could be replaced by Christ, then Christian baptism may be seen as a replacement for circumcision, as well as for Jewish purification rites, which Justin calls the "baptism of wells." This term refers to cisterns in which water was gathered for their rites of purification. Jews did know the importance of those purification rites, but Justin caricatures them as empty wells in this part of the *Dialogue*. Whereas Christian baptism may have evolved from Jewish purification rites, Jewish ritual washings were not the same thing as Christian baptism. The former were repetitive acts whereas the latter was not. Each was administered differently and had different objectives. Justin has rendered them comparable but has done so to demonstrate the superiority of Christian baptism over the supposed ineffectiveness of Jewish purification rites as part of his supersessionist project.

Sabbath

Justin thinks that the laws governing the observance of the Sabbath were required of Israel because of its sins:

> As I stated before, it was by reason of your sins and the sins of your fathers that, among other precepts, God

> imposed upon you the observance of the Sabbath as a sign. (*Dialogue* 21.1)

He takes as his proof text Ezekiel 20:18–26, in which God enjoins Sabbath observance on Israel. The passage, however, does not attribute the origin of Sabbath observance to the fact that Israel had sinned in the past. Rather, God commanded Sabbath observance as a sign of the covenant between God and Israel, and so that Israel would know that God was the Lord their God (Ezek 20:19–20). The subsequent threats of punishment in Ezekiel 20:22–26 were not enforced, so that Israel would know the Lord was also a merciful God. The fidelity of God to Israel is paramount in these texts. Justin changes the original meaning of the texts from Ezekiel to press his point that the Sabbath was commanded of Israel because of its sins, reducing the Sabbath command to a "sign." Justin continues this theme of the institution of Sabbath law because of Israel's sins in *Dialogue* 22–24.

Justin also includes sacrifice and the temple among the Jewish institutions that God commanded because of Israel's sins:

> Thus, your sacrifices are not acceptable to God, nor were you first commanded to offer them because of God's need of them, but because of your sins. The same can be said of the temple, which you refer to as the Temple in Jerusalem. God called it his house or court, not as if he needed a house or a court, but because, by uniting yourselves to him in that place, you might abstain from the worship of idols. (*Dialogue* 22.11)

Justin wrongly assumes that these Jewish institutions were established because of Israel's sins, perhaps unwittingly showing his ignorance of the purpose of the law. It is odd that he would claim that sacrifices were instituted because of Israel's sins when sacrifices were commanded to expiate Israel's sins. He turns a positive command for repentance and sacrifice into something negative that resulted supposedly from Israel's infidelity; he does something similar with the temple in Jerusalem, which he claims was built to put an end to Israel's idolatry. There is no mention of that motivation for building the temple in Solomon's prayer of dedication in 1 Kings 8. In fact, in 1 Kings 8:46–53 Solomon makes clear that the temple is the place where repentance and forgiveness of sins can be attained. Also, it is evident from 1 Kings 11:1–8 that building the temple was not a remedy for idolatry. Ignoring Israel's Scriptures is another form of supersessionism.

If Trypho and other Jews cannot accept Justin's arguments concerning the Sabbath and the temple sacrifices, Justin takes their rejection to be tantamount to denying that the God of the Hebrew Scriptures is the same God worshiped by Christians. For Justin, if God is immutable and if there was a time when people were justified apart from circumcision, Sabbath observance, or temple sacrifices, then there is no need of those institutions after the advent of Christianity. His argument is a *reductio ad absurdum*:

> If we do not accept this conclusion, then we shall fall into absurd ideas, as the nonsense either that our God is not the same God who existed in the days of Enoch and all the others who were not circumcised in the flesh, and did not observe the Sabbaths and the other rites, since Moses only imposed them later; or that God does not wish each succeeding generation of humanity always to perform the same acts of righteousness. Either supposition is ridiculous and preposterous. (*Dialogue* 23.1)

In his view, what made these Jewish institutions unnecessary was the birth of Christ:

> For if circumcision was not required before the time of Abraham, and if there was no need of Sabbaths, festivals, and sacrifices before Moses, they are not needed now, when, in accordance with the will of God, Jesus Christ, his Son, has been born of the Virgin Mary, a descendant of Abraham. (*Dialogue* 23.3)

Moreover, having admitted that Abraham was indeed circumcised, he reinterprets the meaning of his circumcision in a supersessionist way by reducing it to a mere sign:

> Indeed, while Abraham himself was still uncircumcised, he was justified and blessed by God because his faith was in him, as Scriptures tell us. Furthermore, the Scriptures and the facts of the case force us to admit that Abraham received circumcision for a sign, not for justification itself. (*Dialogue* 23.4)

It is curious that Justin does not cite Galatians 3:6–9, where Paul makes a similar argument, albeit one that is not supersessionist. Paul does not spiritualize Abraham's circumcision; rather, he claims that God had justified Abraham based on his trust in God (Gen 15:6) before he commanded him to be circumcised (Gen 17:9–14). Paul's argument is a temporal one. He is speaking to Gentiles, who he believes have already been included among the descendants of Abraham (Gen 12:3; Gal 3:6–9), thus rendering circumcision unnecessary for them. Paul deals only with Abraham and does not speak about other Israelite ancestors who had not been circumcised and were yet pleasing to God. He is not speaking of justification. Justin, however, presses a different point: not only is circumcision not necessary for Christians, but it is not necessary even for Jews. This is without question a supersessionist argument: he denies the importance of circumcision for Jews because he believes it has been replaced by Christian baptism, and he goes so far as to encourage Trypho to receive baptism (*Dialogue* 14.2; 18.2).

The Messiah

In the *Dialogue*, Justin broaches the neuralgic question of the Messiah, his origins, and his identity. The first mention occurs in Trypho's exhortation to Justin to become a Jew by having himself circumcised, observing the Sabbath commands, and fulfilling the entire law—all of which will bring about an awareness of God in him. Trypho then raises a doubt about the existence of the Messiah and levels a charge against Christians who believe that the Messiah has arrived:

> But if the Messiah has been born and exists anywhere, he is not known, nor is he conscious of his own existence, nor has he any power until Elijah comes to anoint him and make him manifest to all. But you [Christians] have believed this foolish rumor, and you have invented for yourselves a Christ for whom you blindly give up your lives. (*Dialogue* 8.3)

Justin responds to Trypho's provocation in the next chapter. He sternly declares that Christians "do not believe in groundless myths nor in teachings not based on reason, but in doctrines that are inspired by the Divine Spirit, abundant with power and teeming with grace" (*Dialogue* 9.1).

A particularly thorny issue for Trypho is the Christian belief in a crucified Messiah, something Jews could not hold. The Messiah's death is foretold in the apocalyptic book of 4 Ezra 7:29, but that is not a death by crucifixion. In presenting his Christian idea of the Messiah, Justin appeals to a different scriptural text. He offers a large block of text from Daniel 7:9–28, which prophesies the coming of the "Son of Man," a title which in the original Aramaic simply meant a human being. Joseph A. Fitzmyer, SJ, has shown that at the time of Daniel's composition this figure was not thought of as a messianic figure.[12] In the New Testament (Mark 14:62; John 1:51) and later Christian literature the Son of Man is a messianic figure. That is exactly how Justin understands the title in *Trypho* 31:1–7. Trypho's retort in the following chapter affirms the future coming of the Son of Man as the great Messiah. This is very interesting because second century CE Jews did not think the phrase "the Son of Man" referred to the Messiah. Either Justin has assimilated Jewish thought in his day to the Christian interpretation of that term, or, as Daniel Boyarin has suggested, some of Justin's views of Judaism may have been supplied by messianic Judaism, which would have accepted Jesus as a crucified Messiah.[13] Curiously, then, Justin has Trypho reject the messianic interpretation of "Son of Man" to distinguish his understanding of Judaism from Christianity. Trypho makes clear that Jews do not accept a crucified messiah:

> Sir your quotations from Scripture prove that we must look forward to that glorious and great Messiah who, as the Son of Man, receives the everlasting kingdom from the Ancient of Days. But the one whom you call Christ [Messiah] was without glory and honor to such an extent that he incurred the last curse of God's law, namely he was crucified. (*Dialogue* 32.1)

Trypho does not accept Christ as the Messiah, which is actually the meaning of *Christos* in Greek. Rather, he identifies Christ as the one Justin *calls* the Messiah. He does this because crucifixion is taken to be a curse from God, and that is incompatible with the notion of a Messiah. Without acknowledging it, Justin's Trypho alludes to Deuteronomy 7:23: "Anyone hung on a tree is under God's curse." "To hang on a tree" was a euphemism for crucifixion. Paul in Galatians 3:13 more positively asserts, "Christ redeemed us from the curse of the law by becoming a curse for us—for it is written, 'Cursed is everyone who hangs on a tree.'" That would have been a perfect retort for Justin, but as in *Dialogue*, 23.4, where he had another opportunity to invoke the Apostle Paul, he does not do that. In fact, he seems to suppress Paul's interpretation of the curse text from Deuteronomy to set up his own argument in the next two chapters in which he will show Trypho's ignorance of a host of scriptural texts that highlight Christ's messiahship. Thus, he casts Judaism in a bad light and reprises his earlier claims that Jews do not know their own Scriptures (*Dialogue* 32–34).

Continuing with the themes of Christ's messiahship and the failure of Trypho to understand the Scriptures, Justin undertakes the problematic text of Isaiah 7:14: "Look, the young woman is with child and shall bear a son and shall name him Immanuel." Jews understood the text to prophesy the birth of the next king in the line of David after Ahaz. His name was Hezekiah, as the reader infers from what Trypho himself claimed about this child (*Dialogue* 69.7). In contrast, Christians, reading the Greek version of the text, understand the "young woman" to be a "virgin," *parthenos* in Greek. And so, the king in the line of David prophesied here is the Messiah, namely, Jesus Christ. Thus, Justin counters:

> "Trypho," I replied, "if this prophecy of Isaiah, Behold, a virgin shall conceive, did not refer to the house of David, but to some other house of the twelve tribes, then the problem would, perhaps, be difficult; but since the prophecy itself refers to the house of David, Isaiah explained exactly how that which was spoken in mystery to David by God would happen.
>
> "Perhaps, my friends, you do not realize that many of the sayings which were expressed mysteriously in metaphorical or obscure language or were hinted at by symbolic actions were later expounded by the prophets who lived after those who had uttered or done them." (*Dialogue* 68.6)

Trypho acknowledges Justin's argument and says he agrees with it, but then Justin questions whether Trypho is not obliged to doubt the Greek translation of the seventy Jewish elders. He accuses Jews of making flawed interpretations such as this one that distorts the text and gives it another meaning.

This is another example of Justin's supersessionist claim that Jews do not know their own Scriptures and that only the Christian interpretation of Scripture is the correct one (*Dialogue* 68.8). Justin revisits this problem of translating Isaiah 7:14 in *Trypho* 71.3 and 84.1. Running through these arguments are the references in which Justin accuses Trypho and his friends of being ignorant of the sacred text in part because they have not had proper teachers who could show them the deeper meaning of it. Christians, however, have supposedly received that proper instruction, thus making Christianity superior to Judaism in the interpretation of the Scriptures. Justin writes,

> "My friends," I replied, I pardon you, and may the Lord forgive you, for you don't know what you are saying; you have been instructed by teachers who are ignorant of the meaning of the Scriptures, and, raving like an oracle, you blurt out whatever comes into your mind. If you will agree to hear our account of him [Christ], how we

> have not been deceived by false teachings, and how we shall not cease to profess our faith in him (even though men thereby persecute us, and the most cruel tyrant tries to force us to deny him), I will prove to you, here and now, that we do not believe in groundless myths nor in teachings not based on reason, but in doctrines that are inspired by the Divine Spirit, abundant with power, and teeming with grace." (*Dialogue* 9.1)

These claims of ignorance of Scripture are like ones made in the *First Apology* and serve a similar purpose.[14] The accusations that the Jews do not understand their own Scriptures challenges the integrity of the Hebrew Bible and renders Judaism inferior to Christianity, which alone possesses the truth of Scripture. Here we have a stock element of supersessionism, namely, that the New Testament is the only authentic interpretation of the oracles and prophecies of the Hebrew Bible. This claim is an unfortunate form of replacing the Jewish scriptural tradition with a Christian one.

Divine Retribution for the Death of Jesus

Justin's treatment of the death of Jesus was prominent in the *First Apology*,[15] and he continues along those same lines in the *Dialogue* in pointed passages that interpret Jewish suffering as divine retribution for the death of Christ. Justin inveighs,

> Indeed the custom of circumcising the flesh, handed down from Abraham, was given to you as a distinguishing mark to set you off from other nations and from us Christians. The purpose of this was that you and only you might suffer the afflictions that are now justly yours; that only your land be desolate, your cities ruined by fire; that the fruits of your land be eaten by strangers before your very eyes; that not one of you be permitted to enter Jerusalem.
>
> Your circumcision of the flesh is the only mark by which you can certainly be distinguished from other men. Nor do I believe that any of you will attempt to

> deny that God either had or has foreknowledge of future events, and that he does not prepare beforehand what everyone deserves. Therefore, the above-mentioned tribulations were justly imposed upon you.
>
> For you have murdered the Just One, and his prophets before him; now you spurn those who hope in him, and in him who sent him, namely almighty God, the Creator of all things; to the utmost of your power you dishonor and curse in your synagogues all those who believe in Christ. Now, indeed, you cannot use violence against us Christians, because of those who are in power, but as often as you could, you did employ force against us. (*Dialogue* 16.2–4)

As noted earlier regarding this text, Justin interprets the command for circumcision as a punishment for Israel's transgressions. That punishment was the separation of Jews from Gentiles and Christians. Other passages from *Dialogue* (see 16.1–6; 67.8–10) suggest that Justin also interprets it as a form of divine retribution for the supposed role the Jews had in the crucifixion of Jesus and the deaths of the prophets before him. Justin acknowledges that Christ's crucifixion was part of the divine plan, but he wrongly blames Jews for it because he believes they did it freely and therefore are deserving of judgment because of it:

> Now forestall any pretext you may offer by saying it was necessary for Christ to be crucified, and that it was necessary that the transgressors belong to your race, and that it could not have been otherwise, I wish to observe that, although God wanted men and angels to follow his will, he nevertheless was pleased to create them with free will to practice virtue, with the faculty of reasoning in order to know him who created them (that is, through whom they passed from the state of non-existence to that of existence), and with a law they should be judged by him, if they do anything contrary to sound reason. Thus,

> unless we quickly repent, we, both men and angels, shall be found guilty of our sins. (*Dialogue* 141.1)

The argument presents a catch-22 situation for the Jews. They were compelled to follow the divine plan when doing so appeared to compromise their free will; but if their free will was not in some way compromised, the plan could not have been fulfilled. In the end, they are condemned for judgment for doing what they were compelled by God to do. Moreover, they are shown to be irrational according to Justin's assessment.

MARCION OF SINOPE

Perhaps the best-known second-century supersessionist is Marcion of Sinope (ca. 85–ca. 160 CE), who, it needs to be stressed, was condemned as a heretic and excommunicated by the Church. He had evidently been a shipowner and the son of the bishop of the Christian community in that locale. He traveled to Rome sometime in the 130s, became a member of the church there, and established himself as a teacher, but he was excommunicated in 144 (according to some legends by his own father) and his donation of 200,000 sesterces was returned. He continued to enjoy a large following and his Marcionite Church was a rival to the Roman Church.[16]

Marcion sought to rid the Scriptures of the influence of the Old Testament. He opposed the God of the Old Testament to the God of the New Testament. He understood the Jewish God to be a God of wrath and retribution, not exhibiting mercy and goodness; the Christian God to be a God of love having the opposite nature, one that is merciful and good. He called the New Testament God the "strange" God, whose son Jesus was sent into the world as its savior.[17]

Marcion's canon of Scripture was short, comprising only the Gospel of Luke in an abbreviated form and ten of the letters of Paul (Gal, 1 and 2 Cor, Rom, 1 and 2 Thess, Eph, Col, Phil, and Phlm).[18] Although his *Antitheses* is no longer extant, around the turn of the twentieth century Adolf von Harnack reconstructed its content from other early Christian writers, mostly from Tertullian's treatise *Against Marcion*. Some of the *Antitheses* can be found in Epiphanius's *Panarion* 42. Marcion's supersessionism is constituted by the fact that he removed the Old Testament from the biblical canon, having rejected the Law and the Prophets, and he reduced the New Testament to that end. Once again, such radical views led to the condemnation of Marcionism as a heresy.

IRENAEUS OF LYONS

Irenaeus was the bishop of Lyons in what was Roman Gaul in the latter part of the second century CE. His best-known work, *Against the Heresies*, mostly targeted what he considered to be false knowledge about Christ by diverse groups of Christians, whom he called "Gnostics." The name derives from the Greek word for knowledge, *gnosis*, which according to the book's subtitle he dubbed "knowledge falsely so-called." Defending what would later become known as orthodox Christianity, Irenaeus created a taxonomy of these movements and their teachers, tracing a genealogy going back to Simon Magus, who first appears in Acts of the Apostles 8:9–24. Irenaeus also engaged in an *Adversus Judaeos* (*Against the Jews*) polemic even before that became formalized as a movement in the fourth century CE.

Like Justin, Irenaeus believed that Jews lacked the proper knowledge of their own Scriptures. In the early part of the fourth book of *Against the Heresies*, Irenaeus proclaimed the unity of God and Christ, so that, against Marcion, there is not a wicked God of the Old and another benevolent God of the New Testament (4.1.1–2; 4.2.1–7). Rather, both the Law and the Prophets proclaimed only one God unified with Christ (4.5.1–6.7), leading Irenaeus to assert that the Jews were mistaken not to receive Christ along with God the Father, something for which Christ himself had supposedly rebuked them. Irenaeus writes,

> To explain, when the Lord manifested himself to his disciples as the Word who makes known the Father and rebuked the Jews who thought that they possessed God, though they even set aside the Word through whom the Father is known, he said, *No one knows the Son except the Father, nor does anyone know the Father except the Son, and anyone to whom the Son chooses to reveal him* [Matt 11:27; Luke 10:22]...they interpret it as if the true God had not been known to anyone before the Lord's coming. They assert, too, that the God who was heralded by the Prophets is not the Father of Christ. (Irenaeus 4.6.1)

A little later, he continues the charge in a similar vein, claiming that the Jews believe they can know the Father apart from the Son:

> Consequently, the Jews apostatized from God by not receiving his word but thinking that they can know the Father himself without the Word, that is, without the Son. (Irenaeus 4.7.4)

Like Justin Martyr before him, Irenaeus sees Christ hidden in the Hebrew Bible, so that when God is revealed in the text so also is Christ. He even expounds as proof of this unity between the Father and Son the same Gospel texts as Justin had: "No one knows the Son except the Father, nor does anyone know the Father except the Son, and anyone to whom the Son chooses to reveal" (Matt 11:27; Luke 10:22; *First Apology* 63.3).

Likewise, in addition to preaching the unity of the Old Testament covenants, Irenaeus insists that God's purpose was the same in the old covenant and the new. Nevertheless, he opposes the law to the Gospel:

> All things, therefore, are from one and the same substance, namely, from one and the same God, as the Lord for his part said to the disciples, "therefore, every scribe who has been trained for the kingdom of heaven is like a householder who brings out of his treasure what is

> new and what is old." He did not teach that one God brought out the old things and another the new; but he was one and the same. For the Lord is the householder who has dominion over the Father's entire home, giving a suitable law to the slaves and those uninstructed; but to the free men and those justified through faith he gives suitable precepts and to the children he opens up the inheritance....Thus, then, the new and the old that are brought out from the storeroom, he, without contradicting himself, calls the two covenants. The old covenant he shows to be the previous Law; the new, the mode of life that is in according to the Gospel." (Irenaeus 4.9.1)

It would have been fine had Irenaeus proclaimed the unity of God in Christ and the unity of the covenants as such for Christians alone. He goes further, however, by drawing a comparison between Judaism and Christianity and invoking the supersessionist saw of servitude versus freedom. The old covenant was suitable for slaves, but the new applies to those freed by Christ. This is expressed in what becomes a standard dichotomy: Judaism and Christianity described as law and Gospel, respectively.

According to Irenaeus,

> "Something greater than the temple is here" [Matt 12:6] he [Christ] said. But "greater" and "less" are not said about things that have nothing in common and are of opposite nature and mutually repugnant, but of things that are of the same substance and have something in common but differ only in quantity and size. For example, water from water, light from light, and grace from grace. So the law that was given for liberty is greater than that which was given for servitude. (Irenaeus 4.9.2)

Irenaeus's conclusion is curious, since his opening sentence suggests the opposite of the conclusion that he draws. If "greater" does not imply opposition of the "greater" to the "lesser," and if the comparison involves things that are of the same substance with properties in common, how can one be better than the other? Are they not simply different? Irenaeus's supersessionist interpretation requires that he subordinate the old covenant to the new covenant, even though they were both authored by one and the same God, and so he ends up violating his own logic. In offering the example of "water from water, light from light, and grace from grace," is he not speaking about the same things? In fact, he does try to show that there is more than a quantitative difference between the old and new covenants. There is a qualitative difference as well in service of maintaining the unity of God with Christ to obviate the problem of the Marcionite distinction between a wrathful God of the Old Testament and a loving God of the New:

> From him [the Father] the Son at his coming did not bring the knowledge of another Father but of the same one who was heralded from the beginning. From him, too, the Son brought liberty for those who rightfully and readily and wholeheartedly serve him. On the contrary, there are the scoffers and those who are not submissive to God but for the sake of praise from men observe outward purifications—which were handed down as types of future things, as if the Law sketched some shadow and delineated the eternal by the temporal, the heavenly by the earthly—they imagined that they observed more than what was prescribed, as though they were more diligent than God himself, whereas within they were full of hypocrisy and of covetousness, and every malice. For those he brought eternal perdition, cutting them off from life. (Irenaeus 4.11.4)

Irenaeus's contrast between the old and new covenants takes on an especially virulent tone toward Jews, whom he portrays as scoffers and as those who are not submissive to God. They observe external purifications which he reduced to "types" that point away from the covenant of servitude toward the covenant of liberty. The qualitative difference between the two is expressed by the old covenant's preoccupation with things temporal and earthly and the new covenant's attention to the eternal and the heavenly. Moreover, Irenaeus adds harsher words denigrating Jews for their pretense to be more diligent than God in their observances, which in his view makes them hypocritical, covetous, malicious, and future recipients of Christ's condemnation to perdition, having been cut off from life. These characterizations establish standard tropes about Jews that comprise supersessionist caricatures of Jews and Judaism.

Irenaeus continues his contrast of slavery and freedom in the matter of sacrifices, stressing the qualitative difference between those of Judaism and those of Christianity.

> Oblations, therefore, as a class were not rejected for there were oblations there [Old Testament], and there are oblations here [New Testament]; there were sacrifices in the People [Israel], and there are sacrifices in the Church. Only the kind has been changed, since, of course, it is no longer offered by servants, but by freemen. The Lord, to be sure, is one and the same, but there was a peculiar character for the servants' oblations, and there is a peculiar character for the freemen's so that the sign of liberty might be shown also by the oblations. For with God nothing is purposeless or without meaning. On that account these [the Jews] dedicated their tithes, but those who received liberty dedicate all their goods to the Lord's services, giving gladly and freely the lesser holding hope for greater things. Here the widow, poor as she is, deposits her entire living into God's treasury. (Irenaeus 4.18.2)

This discussion of sacrifices is starkly prejudicial against Jews and Judaism. Paying attention to the verbs is instructive. Jewish oblations and sacrifices "were," whereas Christian sacrifices "are." Jews "were" servants and Christians are freemen. There "was" a peculiar character for sacrifices offered under the covenant of servitude, whereas there "is" a peculiar character for the sacrifices offered under the covenant of liberty. The tense shifts indicate replacement of Jewish sacrifices with Christian ones, which indicates supersessionism. According to Irenaeus, this characterization did not happen by accident but was intentional on God's part, not "purposeless or without meaning." Moreover, the Jewish sacrifices "were" parsimonious, only one tenth of what could have been offered, whereas Christian sacrifices "are" generous, like the widow's mite given out of her substance not her surplus. Irenaeus is nothing if not consistent in the subordination of Jewish institutions to Christian ones.

Finally, Irenaeus includes one of the more common misunderstandings that has punctuated supersessionism and exacerbated anti-Judaism until it became an anchor of antisemitism even into modern times, namely, that the Jews killed Christ. Irenaeus rails,

> He [Christ] will be found according to their own words, to have been made the occasion of the greatest sin for those who laid hands on him and "who pierced him" [John 19:34]. For if he had not come in that manner, certainly they would not have become the murderers of their Lord; and if he had not sent the Prophets to them, certainly they would not have killed them. (Irenaeus 4.28.3)

Although Irenaeus's principal purpose in *Against the Heresies* was to combat the variety of Gnosticisms he encountered in his day as well as Marcionism, he managed to propagate the supersessionism that had preceded him in the second century CE. Incorporating arguments that are like Justin's about how Jews had misunderstood their own Scriptures or could not find the hidden Christ among them, Irenaeus reaffirmed Justin's view of the unity of God and Christ in both the Old and New Testaments.

MELITO OF SARDIS

Melito of Sardis (d. 190 CE) was a second-century CE apologist in the city of Sardis in Asia Minor. Sardis was an important center of Judaism and was also one of the seven churches that received a letter from Christ in the Book of Revelation (3:1–6). Despite conflicting reports among ancient Christian writers concerning Melito's ecclesiastical status, it is likely that he was a bishop. Eusebius of Caesarea in *Ecclesiastical History* 4.26 attributes some eighteen written works to Melito, including one *Apology*, addressed to the Emperor Marcus Antoninus Verus, and two treatises on the celebration of Easter. Still, there are scholars who maintain that Melito himself was a Jew.

Melito's involvement with supersessionism stems from his having been a Quartodeciman, a moniker taken from the Latin for the number fourteen, *quarta decima*. This was a Christian movement in Asia Minor that celebrated Easter on the Jewish Feast of Passover, which was marked on the fourteenth day of the first Jewish month, Nisan (March–April), as prescribed in Leviticus 23:5. In other locations, Christians celebrated Easter on the first Sunday after the full moon following the spring equinox. A controversy over the correct dating for Easter had arisen and caused a division between the Eastern and Western churches. Those opposing the Quartodecimans accused them of being Judaizers for assimilating Easter to the Passover. This division lasted until the time of the Council of Nicaea in 325 CE, which settled the controversy by adopting the Roman date of Easter for all churches, East and West.

During the Quartodeciman controversy, Melito composed an Easter homily contrasting the old Passover celebration with the new celebration of Easter. He likely wrote it between 160 and 170 CE. Even though he had espoused the more ancient celebration of equating Passover with Easter, which might look like a very Jewish thing to do, his homily is ironically anti-Jewish and supersessionist. He clearly intended to replace the Jewish Passover with Christian Easter. The homily follows the liturgical order of the Easter celebration beginning with the reading of the Passover narrative from the Book of Exodus. Easter itself is described in antithetical terms relating to the "old" and the "new," respectively, Judaism (law) and Christianity (word). Melito opens the homily in a highly stylized way. Melito begins the homily:

1. The Scripture of the exodus of the Hebrews has been
   read,

and the words of the mystery have been declared;
how the sheep was sacrificed,
and how the people was saved,
and how the Pharaoh was flogged by the mystery.

2. Therefore, well-beloved, understand,
how the mystery of the Pascha
is both new and old,
eternal and provisional,
perishable and imperishable,
mortal and immortal.

3. It is old with respect to the law,
new with respect to the word.
Provisional with respect to the type,
yet everlasting through grace.
It is perishable because of the slaughter of the sheep,
imperishable because of the life of the Lord.
It is mortal because of the burial in the ground,
immortal because of the resurrection of the dead.

4. For the law is old,
but the word is new.
The type is provisional,
but grace is everlasting.
The sheep is perishable, but the Lord,
not broken as a lamb but raised up as God,
is imperishable.
For though led to the slaughter like a sheep,
he was no sheep.
Though speechless as a lamb,
neither yet was he a lamb.
For there was once a type, but now the reality has appeared.

5. For instead of the lamb there was a son,
and instead of the sheep a man;
in the man was Christ encompassing all things.[19]

Like other second-century CE apologists, Melito draws qualitative differences between the elements of the Exodus narrative as prescribed by the old law and the newness of the Lamb, Christ, who has replaced the sheep. He also employs typology to strengthen the contrast between the "old" and the "new," where the old prefigures the new as type that is contrasted with reality. He uses fulfillment language here to show how the Easter mystery surpasses the Passover ritual. Whereas the descriptive words of Passover ritual are old, provisional, perishable, mortal, and type, the descriptive words of Easter are new, eternal, imperishable, immortal, and reality. Like other apologists, Melito employs typology to solidify the distinction of old and new. The "type" points to the "reality" but is not equal to it. It is only a preparation for the truth without any legitimate purpose of its own. The "type" has been diminished. These features are typical of supersessionist interpretation.

Later in the homily, he intensifies that sharp contrast by employing the language of destruction. The "type" is not only diminished but is now destroyed because it is useless since the "reality" is all that matters.

> 37. When the thing comes about of which the sketch was a type,
> that which was to be, of which the type bore the likeness,
> then the type is destroyed, it has become useless,
> it yields up the image to what is truly real.
> What was once valuable becomes worthless,
> when what is of true value appears. (Melito, 37)

Although this language continues the contrast between the Passover as a type and Easter as the reality, it is difficult not to imagine Melito extending the meaning here to the differences between Judaism and Christianity. Like Justin, who spoke of the old law and covenant becoming obsolete (*Dialogue* 11.2), of the replacement of worthless circumcision with Christian baptism (*Dialogue* 18.2; 19.2—3), and of Israel itself being replaced by Christianity (*Dialogue* 11.5), so too Melito underscores the destruction of the type: what was once useful is now useless, what was once valued is now worthless. Here we find echoes of the reduction of Jewish ritual to worthless Greek idolatry in the *Epistle of Diognetus* 4.1. as well as the typologies that Irenaeus used to show that Jews do not know the true meaning of their own Scriptures (Irenaeus 4.5.1–6.7; 9.6; 11.4).

Melito, again like other apologists, presents Christ as a replacement for the Jewish law:

> 40. Thus the people [Israel] was a type, like a preliminary sketch
> and the law was the writing of an analogy.
> The Gospel is the narrative and fulfillment of the law
> and the Church is the repository of reality.
>
> 41. So the type was valuable in advance of the reality,
> and the illustration was wonderful before its elucidation.
> So the people were valuable before the Church arose,
> and the law was wonderful before the illumination of the Gospel.
>
> 42. But when the Church arose and the Gospel came to be,
> the type, depleted, gave up meaning to the truth;
> and the law, fulfilled, gave up meaning to the Gospel.
>
> 43. In the same way that the type is depleted,
> conceding the image to what is intrinsically real,
> and the analogy is brought to completion
> through the elucidation of interpretation,
> so the law is fulfilled by the elucidation of the Gospel,
> and the people [Israel] is depleted by the arising of the Church,
> and the model is dissolved by the appearance of the Lord.
> And today those things are worthless,
> since the things of true worth have been revealed. (Melito, 40–43)

These verses are replete with replacement theology in which Christ and the Gospel supersede the Jewish law. Do not these verses tell of the end of Israel and the end of Judaism once Christ has come?

The very dignity and integrity of Jewish Scripture are dissolved apart from the New Testament. The *raison d'être* of the Hebrew Bible ceases to exist in this bishop's mind. Melito's words sound like Irenaeus's comparison of the old law of servitude and the new covenant of liberty.[20]

Like the apologists before him who blamed the death of Jesus on the Jews, Melito follows suit but with an even more extensive treatment of this supersessionist trope:

> 91. For if the king of a nation is seized by enemies
> a war is fought on his account,
> a wall is breached on his account,
> a city is ransacked on his account,
> ransoms are sent on his account,
> envoys are sent off on his account,
> so that he might be brought back alive,
> or buried if he is dead.
>
> 92. But you cast a vote of opposition against your Lord,
> whom the gentiles worshipped,
> at whom the uncircumcised marveled,
> whom foreigners glorified,
> over whom even Pilate washed his hands;
> for you killed him at the great feast.
>
> 93. Therefore the feast of unleavened bread is bitter for you;
> as it is written, "You shall eat unleavened bread with
> bitterness."
> The nails you sharpened are bitter for you,
> the tongue you incited is bitter for you,
> the false witnesses you set up are bitter for you,
> the ropes you prepared are bitter for you,
> the whips which you wove are bitter for you,
> the Judas you hired is bitter for you,
> the Herod you followed is bitter for you,
> the Caiphas you believed is bitter for you,
> the gall you cooked up is bitter for you,
> the vinegar you produced is bitter for you,

the thorns which you gathered are bitter for you,
the hands which you made bloody are bitter for you,
You killed the Lord in the middle of Jerusalem.

94. Listen all you families of the nations and see;
a strange murder has occurred in the middle of Jerusalem; in the city of the law;
in the city of the Hebrews;
in the city of the prophets;
in the city of the righteous.
And who has been murdered? Who is the killer?
I am ashamed to say and I am obliged to tell.
For if the murder took place by night,
and if he was slaughtered in a deserted place,
I might have been able to keep silent.
Now in the middle of the street,
and in the middle of the city,
in the middle of the day before the public gaze,
the unjust murder of a just man has taken place.

95. And so he is lifted up on a tree,
and a placard is attached to show who has been murdered.
Who is it? To say is hard and not to say is more fearful.
Listen then, shuddering at him through whom the earth shook. (Melito, 91–95)

Melito spares no hateful words for the Jews who are the object of his derision. He writes with more hatred than sorrow. The tone is even uglier than that of the apologists who preceded him. The Gospels (Matt 27:33; Mark 15:22; Luke 23:33; John 19:17; see Heb 13:13) show Jesus being crucified outside the city of Jerusalem, but Melito wants his readers or listeners to know that it was in the very heart of Judaism that the Jews supposedly murdered Christ: in the middle of Jerusalem. The repetitive cadence sounds out the drumbeats of his portrayal of the heinous deeds he describes. He includes a dialogue where Israel is questioned about who has been murdered and where, again emphasizing the place: "In the middle of Jerusalem," then drawing out the confession, "I said Israel, I killed the Lord" (Melito, 72–74). Even though Melito decries telling of the murder of Christ, he seems all too happy to relate the story at length in the most gruesome of details.

THE GROWTH OF SUPERSESSIONISM IN THE FOURTH CENTURY

In this survey of the beginnings of Christian supersessionism in the second century we have seen how the apologists aimed to create an identity for Christianity in a religiously pluralistic world. A key element in creating that Christian identity was the construction of Judaism or Judaisms that would render the claims of Christianity superior, or at least credible. We have also seen how hard it is to discern a somewhat historically accurate, recognizable form of Judaism in the constructs created by the apologists. Their "Judaism" was one created in their imagination; it was an imagined Judaism that could easily be replaced by a credible Christianity. That project began in earnest in the second century CE, but it did not end there. It took on another dimension when fed by an imperial impetus and when a sociopolitical asymmetry was introduced between Christianity and Judaism. And so, we turn to the growth of supersessionism in the fourth century and later.

According to Meeks and Wilken, matters began to worsen after the accession of the Emperor Constantine (306–337 CE) in 312 and the issuance of the Edict of Milan in 313 CE, which moved Christianity from being a religion that was at best tolerated to one that was *de facto* the official religion of the Empire.[21] A law issued in 315 CE prevented intermarriages between Christians and Jews. Still, Jews generally fared well under Constantine and any tensions that arose between Christians and Jews had more to do with social and economic changes than with religious conflict. Christians and Jews alike availed themselves of new means of upward mobility under the patronage system in the middle of the fourth century. At the end of that century, however, the fate of Jews would change as a result, somewhat ironically, of the new emperor's favoritism regarding them. Let us consider Antioch as a case study.

Jews and Christians in Fourth-Century Antioch

When the Emperor Julian (dubbed by Christians as "Julian the Apostate") came into power in 361, he moved his residence to Antioch. Having renounced his Christianity, he became a devotee of the local Roman religion. Favoring the Jews, he allied them with the non-Christian population of Antioch to shore up the old traditions and rites of the Roman cults. He thought the Jews could help him in this effort because of their ancient pedigree. To strengthen the alliance with them, he offered to rebuild the temple in Jerusalem and encouraged Jews to resume their own traditional sacrificial practices there. Things did not go as planned. He was unable to restore the temple. Because of their belief that the destruction of the Jerusalem temple was a sign of God's will that the promises made to the Jews would pass to the Christians, Christians interpreted his failure as confirmation, effectively establishing that supersessionist assumption for future generations. Antiochene Christians reacted to Julian's use of the Jews against them by becoming more hostile to them, even to the point of seizing a synagogue and turning it into a church.[22]

John Chrysostom (ca. 347–407)

Animus toward Jews would not cease with that seizure. In 386 CE, John Chrysostom, the eventual archbishop of Constantinople (397 CE), preached eight homilies in Syrian Antioch commonly referred to collectively as *Against the Jews*. Chrysostom did not direct his homilies against Jews per se; rather, he targeted Christians who had become so enamored of Jewish practices that they incorporated them into their own religious lives. Some scholars liken them to Paul's opponents in Galatia and Philippi by calling them "Judaizers." Such subtleties, however, were quickly lost. Even though these homilies were directed toward Christians to get them to renounce Jewish practices, Chrysostom's presentation of Jews was nonetheless vituperative. Marcel Simon, in *Verus Israel*, calls Chrysostom "the master of anti-Jewish invective without question."[23] When his homilies were read in subsequent centuries, their original context took a back seat to his anti-Jewish sentiments.

There is no small irony in the Antiochene Christians' attempts to persuade fellow Christians to adopt Jewish ways. When Paul was a member of the Antiochene church (Acts 13:2), Gentile converts to Jesus Messianism were admitted to it without being circumcised or having to follow the Jewish law. Apparently, this was the practice until some people came from Jerusalem and criticized it (Gal 2:12; Acts 15:1). In response, Paul and Barnabas were appointed to go to Jerusalem to discuss the matter with the apostles and elders there. As we have seen in chapter 1, the resultant compromise was struck whereby Gentiles would not have to undergo circumcision, but they would have to observe the so-called Noahide laws (Gen 9:4)—that is to say, to abstain from eating meat offered to idols, from animals that had been strangled, from consuming the blood of an animal, and from fornication (Acts 15:19–20). We cannot know whether the practices prescribed for Gentile Christians were still in force in Chrysostom's Antioch. But he must have confronted an adoption of Jewish practices of a much wider kind for him to be so adamant against the incorporation of any Jewish customs into Christianity, which included adoption of Jewish feasts and festivals and the return to the practice of circumcision.

The way in which such a prominent Christian as Chrysostom portrayed Jews and Judaism is astonishing. His eight homilies are replete with invective and insult. I offer two examples in order to give a sense of Chrysostom's anti-Jewish sentiments in his *Discourses against Judaizing Christians*.[24]

In the first homily, Chrysostom describes the Judaizing tendencies of his Christian confreres as an illness that infected the Church with certain Jewish feasts and festivals. He inveighs,

> What is this disease? The festivals of the pitiful and miserable Jews are soon to march upon us one after the other and in quick succession: the feast of Trumpets [The New Year], the feast of Tabernacles, the fasts. There are many in our ranks who say that they think as we do. Yet

> some of these are going to watch the festivals and others will join the Jew in keeping their feasts and observing their fasts. I wish to drive this perverse custom from the Church right now. (*Discourses* 1.1.5)

Chrysostom echoes some of the themes that were prominent among the second century CE apologists, such as whether the Jews can really know Christ or recognize his place in their prophetic Scriptures:

> But at any rate the Jews say that they, too, adore God. God forbid that I say that. No Jew adores God! Who says so? The Son of God says so. For he said: "If you were to know my Father, you would also know me. But you neither know me nor do you know my Father." Could I produce a witness more trustworthy than the Son of God? (*Discourses* 1.3.2)

Yet he goes further than the apologists. He questions his coreligionists' loyalty to Christ when they share fasts with those whom he sees as responsible for the death of Christ. Chrysostom thus doubles down on the theme of Jewish deicide:

> But I must get back again to those who are sick. Consider, then, with whom they are sharing their fasts. It is with those who shouted: "Crucify him, Crucify him" with those who said: "His blood be upon us and upon our children." If some men had been caught in the rebellion against their ruler and were condemned, would you have dared to go to them and speak with them? I think not. Is it not foolish, then, to show such readiness to flee from those who have sinned against a man, but to enter into fellowship with those who have committed outrages against God himself? Is it not strange that those who worship the Crucified keep common festival with those who crucified him? Is it not a sign of folly and worst madness? (*Discourses* 1.5.1)

Chrysostom quotes Matthew 27:25 seemingly unaware that the curse pronounced in that text had already expired. In so doing, he propagates the same error as generations of supersessionists: applying the curse to all Jews for all time.

Like the author of *The Epistle of Diognetus* 4.2–6, Chrysostom likens Jewish worship to that of Greek and Roman religion. Both, he argues, are idolatrous:

> So the godlessness of the Jews and the pagans is on a par. But the Jews practice a deceit which is more dangerous. In their synagogue stands an invisible altar of deceit which is more dangerous on which they sacrifice not sheep and calves but the souls of men. (*Discourses* 1.6.4)

Of course, the altar in question must be invisible because synagogues had no altars and sacrifices were not conducted in them. His stress here on deceit, which he repeats in the next section of the Discourse (1.6.5), is a common anti-Jewish trope.

Another clear instance of Chrysostom's supersessionist intent occurs in the seventh homily, in relation to an explication of Hebrews 9:13–14. He claims,

> If the blood of bulls and goats and the sprinkled ashes of a heifer sanctify the unclean for the cleansing of the flesh, how much more will the blood of Christ, who through the Holy Spirit offered himself unblemished, cleanse our conscience from dead works? This gives us abundant proof, then, that those old rituals have stopped, that a new rite has been brought forward to replace them, and that the old will not hereafter be restored. (*Discourses* 7.4.2)

The actual Greek text has "through [an] eternal spirit," which echoes "eternal redemption" in verse 12. Taken together, these two instances of the adjective *eternal* point to the quality and duration of Christ's redeeming death, which the author of Hebrews understood to be solely accomplished by Christ. But Chrysostom used a text with the variant reading "Holy Spirit," who according to Chrysostom mediated Christ's self-offering. Thus, Chrysostom changed the nature of Christ's sacrifice. Whereas it is correct for him to say that the "old rituals have stopped," it is so only if he refers to Jewish sacrifice. As we have seen, Jewish sacrifice ceased after 70 CE, except perhaps at the temple of Leontopolis in Egypt. Chrysostom's claim that they "will not hereafter be restored" was technically correct, but it does not account for the study of Torah, which replaced sacrifice in rabbinic Judaism. The new rite Chrysostom refers to is the death of Christ understood as an atoning sacrifice. Accordingly, for him Christ's death has superseded Jewish sacrifice. This is an example of the supersessionist interpretation of Hebrews.

The *Adversus Judaeos* Tradition in Late Antique and Medieval Christianity

From the fourth century on, widespread supersessionist thought became normative in Christianity. In fact, there is an extensive collection of Christian anti-Jewish tractates extending to the modern period that falls under the heading of *Adversus Judaeos* (*Against the Jews*). A. Lukyn Williams, who has collated anti-Jewish texts from the second through the fourteenth centuries, points out the surprising sameness that characterizes all of them.[25] He demonstrates how one author after another simply repeated the same memes, showing little originality or creativity. Although in some cases authors clearly copied another's work, for the most part there does not seem to have been extensive copying. The frequent repetition of certain themes attests instead to how widespread anti-Judaism was. The supersessionist invective became *de rigueur*. The lack of variation in Christian polemics against Jews should come as no surprise, since the mere repetition of these themes effectively validated their content under the rubric that if something is repeated often enough it becomes a truth of its own. As we have seen, efforts to deny the integrity of the Hebrew Bible were fueled by the repetitive claim that Jews did not understand their own Scriptures. We have seen this claim in Justin Martyr, Irenaeus of Lyons, and Melito of Sardis. Williams argues that such repetition reveals just how little Christians understood the Jewish mind.[26] Williams shows how firmly anti-Judaism was established down through the Middle Ages and how it contributed to the expansion of supersessionism among many Christian authors.

As it is not my intention to present a comprehensive treatment of every instance of supersessionism from the second to the twentieth centuries, I refer readers interested in that longer history to John Pawlikowski's article "Religion as Hatred," which examines the topic of religion as a source of hatred through the lens of antisemitism over a broad swath of history.[27] Pawilowski argues that the *Adversus Judaeos* tradition was a driving force of anti-Jewish hate speech throughout the centuries. It was foundational for later anti-Jewish invective, not only in the realm of religion, but in other social and political realms. In a more recent work, Pawlikowski returns to the *Adversus Judaeos* tradition, which he argues has not been completely eradicated from Catholic Christianity.[28]

CONCLUSION

The chapter has traced the emergence of supersessionism in second-century Christian authors. The texts we looked at move in the direction of an intensifying supersessionism. The debates over identity and self-definition that we saw in the New Testament texts covered in the second chapter metamorphosed into a supersessionism that was external to Judaism; as a part of that process, Judaism was reduced and denigrated to support claims that it was replaced by Christianity. The fact that supersessionist tropes are found in multiple second-century-CE writers with some repetition demonstrates that this replacement theology drew upon a common store of such ideas.

In order to defend Christianity against other religions of their day, the apologists strove to present Christianity as a worthy sparring partner that was actually superior to Greek and Roman religions, especially regarding its philosophical moorings. Their attention to the excellence of Christianity, however, did not stop there. Due to the closeness between Christianity and Judaism in the minds of their deprecators, these apologists felt it necessary to distinguish Christianity from Judaism. In the process of fashioning a distinct identity, Christian authors created a wider distance between these two kindred religions. Even though they shared so much by way of common religious texts, similar ritual practices, traditional ethical demands, and future hopes, supersessionism was pursued by Christian authors to push away their Jewish confreres. The transference of the election of the Jews by God to a new Israel that comprises Christians alone drew a bright line between old and new covenants, resulting in fearful tensions and competition between law and Gospel. The insistence on the part of some Christian thinkers on Jewish blindness in failing to find the prefigured Christ in their own Scriptures and the denial of his status as the Messiah, as well as their challenges to the validity of Jewish rites and customs such as circumcision, feasts, and festivals only drove the wedge in deeper, depriving Jews of their covenantal identity. Relationships between Christians and Jews became increasingly strained, and even the specter of conversion to Christianity was not sufficient to obviate the problem from the Christian perspective. This growing rivalry in the second century was just the beginning of the decline in the relationship between Christians and Jews.

We then turned to fourth-century-CE Syrian Antioch, where the story of Christians and Jews in Antioch is instructive for understanding the growth of anti-Jewish supersessionism in both the Eastern and Western Empire. The establishment of a community in the first century CE, in which Gentiles and Jews could gather without expecting the Gentiles first to become Jews, boded well for the development of Christianity. As time passed and fissures in the relationships between Christians and Jews emerged, the hoped-for harmony between them was threatened by strong anti-Jewish sentiments on the part of certain Christian leaders. By the end of the fourth century, John Chrysostom's homilies against the Christian Judaizers painted a harsh picture of Jews, their worship, and their customs that was to become so embedded in the minds of Christians that it would be very difficult to overcome. What began as an effort to isolate Antiochene Jews and bring right order to the Antiochene Church devolved into open conflict so that by the eighth century CE Jews were expelled from Antioch.[29] The pattern of oppressing Jews was established.

We also briefly examined the emergence of the *Adversos Judaeos* traditions in late antiquity—traditions that continued throughout the Middle Ages, thus solidifying centuries of supersessionist polemics further endangering Jews. These anti-Jewish traditions provide clear examples of how little Christians understood the Jewish mind. Their persistence down through the modern era shows how little Christians cared to learn about the Jewish mind.

In the next chapter, we turn our attention to the twentieth century and the seismic changes that led the Catholic Church to reject without equivocation supersessionism and antisemitism.

Chapter Four

ROMAN CATHOLIC TEACHING ON SUPERSESSIONISM

From the time of the Second Vatican Council in 1965, the Roman Catholic Church has unequivocally condemned supersessionism. As we will see in this chapter, that change in attitude, policy, and teaching concerning Jews and Judaism was a seismic shift away from the centuries-long supersessionism that was characteristic of so much of Christianity. This striking about-face made possible the initiatives taken by Catholic Church leaders from the mid-twentieth century to the present day to repair the damage that supersessionism had done to the relationships with Jews and Judaism. In this chapter, I present the main contours of these monumental shifts leading up to Vatican II and then emanating from it. As a point of reference throughout, I trace the saga of the Good Friday Prayer and calls, both internal and external, for its rewording when it came to how it describes the Jews.

THE EARLY AND MID-TWENTIETH CENTURY

The first half of the century did not witness any major official change in the Church's view of its relationship to Jews and

Judaism, although behind the scenes there were people and movements urging change. The opening of what was once known as the Vatican Secret Archive (the Latin *secretum* means "private") and is now known as the Vatican Apostolic Archive has given historians fuller access to important documentation for each pontificate in the modern era. In 2002, Pope John Paul II opened the archive for the pontificate of Pius XI (1922–1939). In 2020 Pope Francis opened the archive for the pontificate of Pius XII (1939–1958).

Germany after the First World War

World War I took a devastating toll on all of Europe, of course. In Germany, that devastation would prepare the way for the rise of National Socialism and Adolf Hitler. Germany had lost an estimated 2.4 million dead, with another 4.8 million wounded. In addition to those losses was the humiliation of having lost the war and the punitive measures dictated in the Treaty of Versailles (1919). The reparations that were to be paid, the acceptance of guilt for the war itself, and the loss of significant lands left many Germans resentful, in despair, and dislocated. Demilitarization left Germany vulnerable to invasion with few resources to defend itself. The economic conditions of the fragile Weimar Republic—with its high inflation and loss of natural resources, shortage of jobs, and prohibitive cost of food and goods—contributed to economic catastrophe. Various paramilitary groups vied for influence and power in cities. Historians theorize that the social unrest in Germany in the aftermath of the war and the horrid conditions of life that it had wrought were enough to seek the blame for all the problems on people other than the Germans. The Communists and the Jews became easy scapegoats, even though they had fought bravely for their country in the war. When Hitler assumed power as chancellor in 1933, he enacted many measures against both groups to limit their place in German society. Antisemitism spread as the Jews were blamed for Germany's having lost the war.

It was not long before plans emerged among the Nazis to eradicate Jews completely from Germany and other European nations. Influenced by currents of social Darwinism, the Nazi Party declared that the Aryan race is the master race of humanity and sought to protect its purity at all costs. Beginning in 1933, Hitler and his regime tried to purge Germany of non-Aryan peoples and of anyone they labeled as subhuman and genetically inferior. Jews, Slavs, Roma, homosexuals, the disabled, the mentally ill, and anyone who suffered from congenital illnesses were all targeted. In 1935 the Nuremburg Laws were passed (although they were not fully enacted until after the Berlin Olympics in 1936). Racial mixing was thereby prohibited in Nazi Germany and every measure was taken to eradicate people who were considered racially impure. Embracing eugenics, the Nazis regularly practiced forced sterilization and euthanasia. After the invasion of Poland in September 1939, ghettos were created to isolate the Jews. Concentration camps were created to imprison millions of people destined for mass murders. In January 1942, top-ranking Nazi and government officials met to plan and implement the elimination of European Jews (The Wannsee Conference). "The Final Solution" was a euphemism for a Nazi culture of death that refined horrid methods of killing to exterminate as many people as possible.

Pius X (1903–1914) and Anti-Modernism

In the early twentieth century the Catholic Church was divided over the Jewish question. Those divisions largely reflected other divisions within the Church that had been precipitated by the French Revolution. As John O'Malley, SJ, explains it in *What Happened at Vatican II*,[1] not only had the French Revolution shaken and temporarily abolished the monarchies on the Continent, but in so doing it had also shaken to its foundation the old marriage of throne and altar, that is, state support of the Catholic Church to the exclusion of all others. Even more devastating was the ideology that carried these events forward. Behind the Revolution lay the Enlightenment, which on the Continent was rabidly anticlerical, often anti-Christian, and especially anti-Catholic.

Thus, within the Church there were, on the one side, monarchist currents that resisted the new historical consciousness and democratic ideals and, on the other side, liberal currents that were more open to the modern world. The history of this era in the Church is what O'Malley refers to as "The Long Nineteenth

Century"—*long* because it did not end until the Second Vatican Council in the 1960s. The story of the Church's position on supersessionism and its unequivocal rejection of it in *Nostra Aetate* (1965) is best understood against this backdrop.

At the turn of the twentieth century, there were within the Vatican many conservatives opposed to admitting *any* changes in the Church teachings and rituals, including its view of Jews and Judaism. These were largely clerics who were anti-Modernists. *Modernism* was a term used to describe theological views and methods that emerged in the nineteenth and early twentieth centuries. It was promoted by theologians who wanted to present the Catholic faith to the faithful in an appropriate forward-looking manner. As O'Malley puts it, the desire of the so-called Modernists was "to help the church reconcile itself with what they felt was best in intellectual culture as it had evolved into the present."[2] They wanted to be free to employ the new historical consciousness in their study of doctrine (the development of doctrine) and of Scripture (the historical-critical method). Yet, it was not just about scholarship; it also had a political dimension. Some of the Modernists "saw democracy as the system to which society had evolved."[3] Pope Pius X condemned the Modernists. On July 3,1907, he issued the decree *Lamentabili Sane Exitu* (With Lamentable Results) against the people involved. Two months later, he issued *Pascendi Dominici Gregis* (Feeding the Lord's Flock), in which he declared "Modernism" a heresy. Beginning in 1910, he required that "all clergy, pastors, confessors, preachers, religious superiors, and professors in philosophical-theological seminaries" take the Oath Against Modernism (*Sacrorum Antistitum*). In the end, however, such reactionism would not hold.

Pius XI (1922–1939), Antisemitism, and the Good Friday Prayer

In 1926, a group favoring improvement of relations with the Jews, called the *Opus Sacerdotale Amici Israel* (Clerical Association of Friends of Israel), was founded. Its membership included nineteen cardinals, two hundred eighty-seven bishops, and three thousand priests. The group's purpose was to oppose antisemitism and foster a more positive view of Jews among Catholics. It also promoted the conversion of Jews to Catholicism. The *Amici Israel* petitioned Pope Pius XI to alter the language of the intercessory prayer for the conversion of Jews that had included unfortunate mistranslations of two Latin words: *perfidis* and *perfidiam*. There were nine intercessory prayers, the eighth of which was for the conversion of the Jews. The other prayers would be interrupted by the deacon, who would instruct the congregation to genuflect briefly and then to stand; this action would be followed by a concluding prayer. There was, however, no genuflection in the prayer for the conversion of the Jews. Instead, there was an explanatory note: "the genuflection is omitted because of the abhorrence of the insult offered by the Jews to our Savior when they knelt before him in derision in the hall of Pilate's palace." Of course, there is no account of Jews doing that in the Gospels. It was the Roman soldiers who mocked Jesus. The formulation of the prayer for the conversion of Jews was especially hateful:

> Let us pray also for the *perfidious* Jews, that Almighty God may remove the veil from their hearts; so that they too may acknowledge Jesus Christ our Lord. Almighty and eternal God, who dost not exclude from thy mercy even Jewish *perfidy*: hear our prayers, which we offer for the blindness of that people; that acknowledging the light of thy Truth, which is Christ, they may be delivered from their darkness. Through the same Jesus Christ our Lord, who lives and reigns with you in the unity of the Holy Spirit, God, for ever and ever. Amen.[4] (emphasis mine)

The Latin words translated as *perfidis* and *perfidiam* should be translated as "unbelieving" and "unbelief"; the English "perfidious" carries a far more negative connotation.[5]

In 1928, Pope Pius XI responded positively to the request of the *Amici Israel* by asking the Sacred Congregation of Rites to reform the text of that prayer. Yet the secretary of the Holy Office,

Cardinal Rafael Merry Del Val, denied the request in language that was antisemitic. He explained:

> The request put forward by the so-called Amici Israel strikes me as completely unacceptable, indeed even rash. We are dealing with ancient prayers and rites of the liturgy of the Church, a liturgy inspired and consecrated for centuries that includes condemnation of the rebellion and betrayal perpetrated by the chosen people who were at once unfaithful; and deicide....I would hope that these Amici Israel would not fall into a trap laid by the Jews themselves, who insinuate themselves throughout modern society and seek with whatever means to minimize the memory of their history and take advantage of the good will of Christians.[6]

In addition to opposing changes to the prayer, the conservatives sought to have the *Amici Israel* suppressed. Pius XI was displeased by the congregation's response but felt forced to accept it. In March 1928 he approved a decree ordering the suppression of the *Amici Israel.* Nevertheless, because of his opposition to antisemitism, he included the following wording in the decree of suppression:

> Just as the Holy See condemns hatred and animosity between peoples, so must it above all condemn hatred against a people already chosen by God, namely that hatred that today is commonly referred to as anti-Semitism.[7]

During the papacy of Pius XI, concern for the persecution of Jews was not a priority, at least not as much as combatting Communism, which the Church saw as its worst enemy. In reaction to Germany's violations of the Reich Concordat, which the Vatican had signed in 1933, Pius XI issued the encyclical *Mit brennender Sorge* (With Burning Concern) in 1937. The German title is notable for the way it broke with the Vatican tradition of titling encyclicals in Latin. The encyclical condemned Nazi ideology and practices, albeit without mentioning the words *National Socialism* or *Nazi.*[8]

Its language was veiled for fear of inciting a strong reaction from the Nazis against Catholics and the Church. The encyclical mostly addressed the plight of German Catholics and clergy living under the Nazi regime; it did not address the plight of Jews, who are nowhere mentioned in it. It exhorted German Catholics to hold fast to faith in God and not to adopt the "pantheistic confusion" holding sway in its place. Pius warned of the danger of the eternal cost of "spiritual loss" and exhorted Catholics that "there is but one alternative left, that of heroism"[9] (21). The encyclical had to be smuggled into Germany, where 300,000 copies were printed so that it could be read from the pulpits of German Catholic churches on Palm Sunday, which fell on March 21 that year.

To his credit, Pius XI was known to oppose racism and anti-semitism. Emma Fattorini in *Hitler, Mussolini, and the Vatican* tells the story of the missing encyclical against racism and anti-semitism.[10] In the summer of 1938, the pope was so impressed by the book *Interracial Justice* authored by the American Jesuit John LaFarge that he invited LaFarge to write an encyclical explicitly condemning racism and antisemitism. LaFarge accepted the invitation, but he did not feel up to writing it himself. Two additional Jesuits, Gustav Grundlach and Gustave Desbuquois, were therefore assigned to assist him. LaFarge sent the finished encyclical to the Jesuit superior general, Wlodzimier Ledóchowski, for delivery to the pope. For some unknown reason, Ledóchowski delayed giving the encyclical to Pius XI for four months, not delivering it until January 21, 1939. Twenty days later Pius died, and the encyclical was never published.[11] Fattorini speculates that Ledóchowski, a staunch anti-Communist, was a supporter of another encyclical of Pius XI, *Divini Redemptoris*, which condemned Communism. He had little interest in the publication of an encyclical condemning antisemitism.[12]

Fattorini tells of another instance when Pius XI condemned antisemitism. After Mussolini decreed his racial laws in September 1938, Pius gave a radio address on Belgian Catholic Radio in which he addressed the fact that Jewish students were banished from Italian public schools. He emphasized the spiritual descent of Catholics from Abraham:

> Abraham is our patriarch, our ancestor. Antisemitism is not compatible with the sublime thought and reality evoked by this text. Antisemitism is a hateful movement with which we as Christians must have no involvement.... Christians are not permitted to take part in antisemitism. We recognize that everyone has a right to self-defense and can undertake those actions necessary to protect his legitimate interests. But antisemitism is inadmissible. Spiritually we are all Semites.[13]

Notice how embedded in this strong rejection of antisemitism is a rejection of supersessionism.

When it came to Nazi Germany, Catholics were varied in the ways they reacted to the treatment of the Jews. There were brave Catholics who resisted National Socialism; some of those risked their own lives to provide Jews with safe transit out of the country, and the intellectual elite among them drew from the Catholic moral and theological tradition to guide them; many were themselves martyred. There were other Catholics who remained silent in the face of Nazi oppression. Still others shamefully embraced Nazi ideology, and the intellectual elite among them abetted Nazi racial antisemitism under the guise of writing scientific and theological treatises. For instance, Georg Bichlmair, the Jesuit Provincial of Austria, preached sermons in Vienna claiming that Jews who converted to Catholicism had defective genes because they had rejected Christ, and that baptism could not repair them.[14]

Pius XII (1939–1958), the Shoah, and the Good Friday Prayer

Eugenio Pacelli was elected pope in 1939. He had been the papal nuncio (ambassador) to Bavaria under Pope Benedict XV (1914–1922) and Cardinal Secretary of State under Pope Pius XI. He was instrumental in negotiating the Reich Concordat between Germany and the Vatican in 1933. Unfortunately, he was overly circumspect about confronting the Nazis, mostly out of concern for German Catholics and the status of Catholicism in the Third

Reich. The question of what Pius XII did or did not do to protect Jews during the Holocaust remains highly contentious. With the recent opening of the apostolic archive for his papacy, we have more evidence of just how little he did to address antisemitism and to advocate for Jews and Judaism. As a marker of that, let us consider his response when, in the immediate wake of the end of World War II, he was petitioned by Jews to alter the Good Friday prayer for their conversion.

David I. Kertzer and Robert Benedetti in "In the Wake of the Holocaust" tell the story of how in March 1945, the newly converted and baptized former Chief Rabbi of Rome, Israel Zolli, met with Pius XII and urged him to change the Good Friday prayer's language.[15] They also mention others, such as Leon Kubowitzki, the Secretary General of the World Jewish Congress, who asked the pope to issue an encyclical condemning antisemitism. One year later, Kubowitzki met with the French ambassador to the Holy See, the theologian Jacques Maritain, who shared the concern that the Church's demonization of Jews had enabled the Holocaust. Kubowitzki conveyed to Maritain his interest in encouraging the pope to write the encyclical against antisemitism. Maritain replied that he himself had urged Pius XII and Monsignor Montini (later to become Pope Paul VI) to do just that, but he suspected that Pius XII and Montini were afraid to undertake such an endeavor. He then reminded Kubowitzki how disappointed he was by the pope's silence during the war concerning the plight of the Jews, and by how the pope avoided the subject except in "roundabout statements."[16]

Kertzer and Benedetti also tell of the saga of Massimo Adolfo Vitale, an Italian Jewish leader who tried to ascertain the fate of thousands of Jews who had been deported from Italy to Nazi concentration camps.[17] Vitale was another leader who hoped to get the wording of the Good Friday prayer changed because he felt it contributed to hatred against Jews. Toward this end, he carried on a long correspondence with the Vatican. It was actually his brother Enrico who first wrote to Pius XII in September 1947, calling on him not only to change the prayer but also to issue a condemnation of antisemitism. Pius XII sent the letter to Father Giuseppe Lörn, a theological consultant to the Vatican's Congregation of Rites, to solicit his opinion on the matter. After tracing the origin of the prayer back to the fifth century, Lörn contended that the wording of such an ancient prayer could not be changed. He offered a weak justification for the refusal by saying that, regardless of the language, the Church was still praying for the Jews and has called upon Christians not to hate the Jews but to pray in a Christian manner for their conversion.

Kertzer and Benedetti recount how the Vitale brothers did not give up on their cause but redoubled their efforts.[18] They were given a ray of hope in June 1948 when the Congregation of Rites issued a declaration that the words in question should correctly be translated "unbelievers" and "disbelief." However, the declaration lacked a mandate to change the wording, and so the words remained in the prayer. In December 1952, Massimo wrote to Pius XII expressing his disappointment that the offending words had not been changed. Monsignor Montini got into the act by sending Massimo's letter to the deputy of the Congregation of Rites, Leonida Dante. Dante replied that the Congregation of Rites had no authority to change the wording of the prayer and that it could only be altered by local bishops. That did not deter Massimo Vitale. Between April 1953 and December 1957, he wrote fifteen letters to the Vatican's Deputy Secretariat of State, Monsignor Angelo Dell'Acqua. They concerned mostly the Good Friday prayer, but in these letters, Massimo also reported incidents of priests preaching antisemitic sermons in several Italian dioceses. The monsignor tried to appear cordial and sympathetic to Massimo regarding his concerns, but he basically stalled the process of repairing the problem of the prayer. He often reassured Massimo, incorrectly, that everything possible was being done to address the wording of the prayer and investigate the antisemitic sermons. At times he cautioned his staff colleagues not to put anything in writing but rather to communicate with Massimo only by telephone. The sad saga ended with the death of Pius XII on October 9, 1958.

Divino Afflante Spiritu (1943)

O'Malley emphasizes the importance of Pius XII's 1943 encyclical, *Divino Afflante Spiritu* (Inspired by the Divine Spirit), in which he very strongly endorsed the "literary, philological, and historical methods of biblical exegesis that had been developing since the nineteenth century."[19] The encyclical was prepared by the German Jesuit and Rector of the Pontifical Biblical Institute Augustin Bea, who, as we shall see, was instrumental in the drafting of *Nostra Aetate* during Vatican II. By endorsing these modern methods of biblical interpretation, the encyclical "dismissed" the allegorical method that had been the mainstay of supersessionist exegesis since the second century CE. Now, the literal sense of Scripture would have priority over the allegorical sense. And so, *Divino Afflante Spiritu* opened the way for the Church's understanding of Scripture and revelation that would be codified in the Dogmatic Constitution on Divine Revelation, *Dei Verbum* (The Word of God), at the Second Vatican Council.

In a Christmas Eve radio address the following year, Pius XII proclaimed that "the future belongs to democracy." He explained, "Taught by bitter experience, people today increasingly oppose monopolies of power that are dictatorial, accountable to no one, and impossible to reject. They want a system of government more compatible with the dignity and the liberty due to citizens."[20] Although when it came to theology the anti-Modernist forces remained powerful, this twofold embrace of the historical-critical method and of democracy signaled a significant shift that presaged the Second Vatican Council.

Pope John XXIII (1958–1963) and the Good Friday Prayer

Kertzer and Benedetti show that, with the election of Pope John XXIII, Massimo Vitale hoped that he would find a sympathetic pontiff who might finally address the problems with the Good Friday prayer.[21] He wrote to the new pope and described the effect that the prayer had on Jews and how it enabled antisemitism among Catholics. On March 27, 1959, Pope John XXIII revisited the issue of the Good Friday intercessory prayer and ordered that the words *perfidious* and *perfidy* be removed. The revised version read as follows:

> Let us pray also for the Jews, that the Lord our God may take the veil from their hearts; so that they also may acknowledge Jesus Christ our Lord. Let us pray: Almighty and everlasting God, You do not refuse Your mercy even to the Jews; hear the prayers, which we offer for the blindness of that people so that they may acknowledge the light of Your truth, which is Christ, and be delivered from their darkness.[22]

Though better than the previous version, critics of the new text were not comfortable with the tone of the rewording insofar as it still perpetuated old prejudices by referring to veiled hearts, blindness, and darkness, and it still called for the conversion of Jews. The good news is that this attempt was not the end of the story for this prayer.

The prayer was once again revised for inclusion in the Good Friday rite as prescribed by the 1970 edition of the Roman Missal under Pope Paul VI. This time the associations are all positive, no longer playing into old tropes:

> Let us pray for the Jewish people, the first to hear the word of God, that they may continue to grow in the love of his name and in faithfulness to his covenant. Almighty and eternal God, long ago you gave your promise to Abraham and his posterity. Listen to your Church as we pray that the people you first made your own may arrive at the fullness of redemption. We ask this through Christ our Lord. Amen.[23]

The judicious wording in this version of the prayer seems finally to have addressed the shortcomings of previous versions. Still another bump in the road occurred in July 2007 under Pope Benedict XVI. Before we get to that part of the story, however, we need to understand the sea change brought about by the Second

Vatican Council, especially when it came to the problem of supersessionism.

THE SECOND VATICAN COUNCIL

Fortunately, a more positive direction in the relationship of Catholics and Jews emerged with the election of Angelo Giuseppe Roncalli to the papacy on October 28, 1958. Three months later, on January 25, 1959, the new Pope John XXIII called for an ecumenical council to help guide the Church into the modern world. John spoke of the Church's need for *aggiornamento*, the Italian word for "updating," and *ressourcement*, the French word meaning "a return to the sources." One area of the Church's life that needed urgent updating was its relationship to Jews and Judaism, especially after the Shoah. The return to the sources, especially to Scripture, would aid in that task. The Second Vatican Council, which met four times between 1962 and 1965, issued several momentous documents, three of which especially changed Roman Catholicism's understanding of Judaism and attitude toward Jews.

Its Declaration on Religious Liberty (1965), *Dignitatis Humanae* (The Dignity of the Human Person), affirms the dignity of every human person based on the revelation that we are created in the image of God, and on the corollary that therefore faith is a matter of conscience and cannot be coerced. It states, "The act of faith is by its very nature a free act" (§10).[24]

Another crucial council document, The Dogmatic Constitution on the Church entitled *Lumen Gentium* (Light of Nations), promulgated a year earlier in 1964, affirms that the covenant with the Jews was never revoked:

> 16. Finally, those who have not yet received the Gospel are related in various ways to the people of God. In the first place we must recall the people to whom the testament and the promises were given and from whom Christ was born according to the flesh [Rom 9:4–5]. On account of their fathers this people remains most dear to

> God, for God does not repent of the gifts He makes nor of the calls He issues [see Rom 11:28–29].[25]

Lumen Gentium and the Declaration on Non-Christian Religions, *Nostra Aetate*, finally rejected supersessionism and antisemitism in unequivocal terms.

Nostra Aetate (1965)

The Council's Declaration *Nostra Aetate* (In Our Age) took up the question of the Church's relation to non-Christian religions. O'Malley puts the matter bluntly:

> Few issues ignited such bitter controversy both inside and outside the council as the relationship of the church to the Jews, and then to other non-Christian religions. Few of the documents, that is to say, bumped along on such a rough road as *Nostra Aetate*. The relationship of the Catholic Church to other Christian churches and communions also had a rough ride, but not nearly so rough as the relationship to the Jews.[26]

The largest section of *Nostra Aetate* (§4) addresses the necessary connection between the people of the new covenant and the descendants of Abraham.

This section on the Church's relation to the Jews had an interesting genesis. On June 13, 1960, Pope John met with the Jewish scholar Jules Isaac, who had survived the Shoah. Isaac had written an important book, *Jésus et Israël*, first published in French in 1948 and in English as *Jesus and Israel* in 1971. Their meeting was arranged at the request of the president of France, Vincent Auriol, through the French Ambassador to the Holy See, Guy de la Tournelle. Isaac's book included a series of twenty-one propositions that demonstrated how the Church's view of Jews and their punishment for their purported role in the death of Christ were fallacious. Isaac brought with him a list of ten recommendations from the International Conference of Christians and Jews, which had convened in Switzerland in 1947 to address antisemitism. The recommendations listed issues that Christian churches (Catholic and Protestant) needed to address in their teachings on Judaism. Isaac hoped that these issues would be taken up at the Council. In his comprehensive account of the origin and history of *Nostra Aetate*, John Borelli notes that, had it not been for this meeting between Pope John and Jules Isaac, *Nostra Aetate* might never have been written.[27]

Nostra Aetate, while the shortest of the Vatican II documents, was subject to considerable discussion and editing through several drafts by the Council's preparatory commissions. Paulist Father Thomas Stransky, an expert on *Nostra Aetate*, characterized it as the document least debated inside the council's hall and the most debated outside. It was carefully shepherded through numerous revisions by Cardinal Augustin Bea, SJ. In 1960 John XXIII appointed him to head the new Secretariat for Promoting Christian Unity, on which Stransky served as part of the staff until 1970. Having been charged with handling the ecumenical matters of the Council, this secretariat was also entrusted with handling the matter of the Church's relations with Jews.[28]

Leo Lefebure in *True and Holy* observes that *Nostra Aetate* was "for Catholics the most dramatic and influential of the official church statements" due to the ways it "radically revised centuries of Catholic teaching about the Jewish people."[29] It was promulgated by Pope Paul VI on October 28, 1965. Despite considerable crises and opposition behind the scenes, *Nostra Aetate* received overwhelming approval. When the final vote was taken, there were 2,221 votes for the schema and 88 against.

Its five relatively short sections address the Church's relationship with all non-Christian religions, but it explicitly mentions only Hinduism, Buddhism, Islam, and Judaism. In this declaration, the Council recognizes the unity of all people who yearn for the One God who is their origin and destiny (§1). It exhorts the Church itself to enter dialogue and collaboration with the followers of other religions, something that had not been encouraged in previous generations of Catholics (§2). It underscores how the Church regards Moslems with respect (§3). And, in its longest section, it addresses the Church's relationship to the Jews, identified as "Abraham's stock" (§4). I quote here in full sections 4 and 5:

> 4. As the sacred synod searches into the mystery of the Church, it remembers the bond that spiritually ties the people of the New Covenant to Abraham's stock.
>
> Thus the Church of Christ acknowledges that, according to God's saving design, the beginnings of her faith and her election are found already among the Patriarchs, Moses and the prophets. She professes that all who believe in Christ—Abraham's sons according to faith [Gal. 3:7]—are included in the same Patriarch's call, and likewise that the salvation of the Church is mysteriously foreshadowed by the chosen people's exodus from the land of bondage. The Church, therefore, cannot forget that she received the revelation of the Old Testament through the people with whom God in His inexpressible mercy concluded the Ancient Covenant. Nor can she forget that she draws sustenance from the root of that well-cultivated olive tree onto which have been grafted the wild shoots, the Gentiles [Rom. 11:17–24]. Indeed, the Church believes that by His cross Christ, Our Peace, reconciled Jews and Gentiles, making both one in Himself [Eph. 2:14–16].
>
> The Church keeps ever in mind the words of the Apostle about his kinsmen: "theirs is the sonship and the glory and the covenants and the law and the worship and the promises; theirs are the fathers and from them is the Christ according to the flesh" (Rom. 9:4–5), the Son of the Virgin Mary. She also recalls that the Apostles, the Church's mainstay and pillars, as well as most of the early disciples who proclaimed Christ's Gospel to the world, sprang from the Jewish people.
>
> As Holy Scripture testifies, Jerusalem did not recognize the time of her visitation [Luke 19:14], nor did the Jews in large number, accept the Gospel; indeed not a few opposed its spreading [Rom. 11:28]. Nevertheless, God

holds the Jews most dear for the sake of their Fathers; He does not repent of the gifts He makes or of the calls He issues—such is the witness of the Apostle. In company with the Prophets and the same Apostle [Rom. 11:28–29], the Church awaits that day, known to God alone, on which all peoples will address the Lord in a single voice and "serve him shoulder to shoulder" (Zeph. 3:9) [Is. 66:23; Ps. 65:4; Rom. 11:11–32].

Since the spiritual patrimony common to Christians and Jews is thus so great, this sacred synod wants to foster and recommend that mutual understanding and respect which is the fruit, above all, of biblical and theological studies as well as of fraternal dialogues.

True, the Jewish authorities and those who followed their lead pressed for the death of Christ [John 19:6]; still, what happened in His passion cannot be charged against all the Jews, without distinction, then alive, nor against the Jews of today. Although the Church is the new people of God, the Jews should not be presented as rejected or accursed by God, as if this followed from the Holy Scriptures. All should see to it, then, that in catechetical work or in the preaching of the word of God they do not teach anything that does not conform to the truth of the Gospel and the spirit of Christ.

Furthermore, in her rejection of every persecution against any man, the Church, mindful of the patrimony she shares with the Jews and moved not by political reasons but by the Gospel's spiritual love, decries hatred, persecutions, displays of anti-Semitism, directed against Jews at any time and by anyone.

Besides, as the Church has always held and holds now, Christ underwent His passion and death freely, because of the sins of men and out of infinite love, in order that all may reach salvation. It is, therefore, the burden of the Church's preaching to proclaim the cross of Christ as the sign of God's all-embracing love and as the fountain from which every grace flows.

> 5. We cannot truly call on God, the Father of all, if we refuse to treat in a brotherly way any man, created as he is in the image of God. Man's relation to God the Father and his relation to men his brothers are so linked together that Scripture says: "He who does not love does not know God" (1 John 4:8).
>
> No foundation therefore remains for any theory or practice that leads to discrimination between man and man or people and people, so far as their human dignity and the rights flowing from it are concerned.
>
> The Church reproves, as foreign to the mind of Christ, any discrimination against men or harassment of them because of their race, color, condition of life, or religion. On the contrary, following in the footsteps of the holy Apostles Peter and Paul, this sacred synod ardently implores the Christian faithful to "maintain good fellowship among the nations" (1 Peter 2:12), and, if possible, to live for their part in peace with all men [Rom. 12:18], so that they may truly be sons of the Father who is in heaven [Matt. 5:45].[30]

There are very important claims and reminders in this section of *Nostra Aetate* by which the Church acknowledges its past failings. I summarize them here:

1. Catholics and Jews are spiritually united with one another.
2. The origins of the Church, its faith and election, are found in the Hebrew Scriptures.
3. Catholics and Jews share the promises of Abraham.
4. The Church received the revelation of the Old Testament through the Jewish people with whom God had made the covenant.
5. The Church is sustained by the root of the olive tree, Judaism, onto which the Gentiles had been grafted as wild shoots.
6. The Church cherishes St. Paul's assessment of the Jewish people in Romans 9:4–5, which recounts the many blessings they have received from God.

7. Jesus, his apostles, and his early followers were Jews.
8. God loves the Jews and does not regret the gifts God bestows on them.
9. The Church awaits the day on which all peoples will address the Lord in a single voice and "serve him shoulder to shoulder."
10. Christians and Jews share a spiritual patrimony that demands mutual understanding, respect, shared biblical and theological study, and dialogue.
11. The Church must not present Jews as rejected or accursed by God.
12. The Church's preaching and teaching about Jews must be truthful and not distorted.
13. The Church decries hatred, persecutions, and any forms of antisemitism directed against Jews at any time and by anyone.
14. Jews should not bear the charge of deicide, and the Church must proclaim the death of Christ as a sign of God's love and the fountain from which all grace flows.

It should come as no surprise that fifteen of the twenty-one propositions about Catholicism's historical misunderstanding of Judaism found in Jules Isaac's book *Jésus et Israël* and discussed by Isaac and Pope John XXIII are addressed in the fourteen items on the above list of claims and reminders found in *Nostra Aetate.* This demonstrates just how seriously John XXIII, Paul VI, and Cardinal Bea took Isaac's concerns about the relationship between Catholics and Jews. Isaac, therefore, was a catalyst in bringing about this dramatic shift in the Catholic Church's teaching on Jews and Judaism. Monsignor Loris Capovilla, a close confidante of John XXIII, recalled the impact that Isaac had on John XXIII:

> Until that day it had not occurred to John XXIII that the Council had to deal with the Jewish question and antisemitism. But from that day on he was completely taken by it.[31]

It must be said that in its condemnation of anti-Jewish hatred and antisemitism, *Nostra Aetate* made an important contribution to the larger mission of social justice in the Catholic Church. David Hollenbach in *Human Rights in a Divided World: Catholicism and a Living Tradition* summarizes the significance of the Second Vatican Council's promotion of social justice: "Because of these dynamic developments in the tradition of Catholic social thought, since Vatican II the Church has in fact become a global leader in the defense of human rights."[32] *Nostra Aetate* should be counted among those "dynamic developments."

The reception of *Nostra Aetate* was not completely smooth. It took some time to enact the document's recommendation for "dialogues and cooperation with the followers of other religions" (§2). Despite its revolutionary character in making this recommendation, *Nostra Aetate* also includes some phrases that echoed the religious supremacy of Christianity from the past. For example, the second section speaks of a ray of truth found in other religions but goes on to cite the portrayal of Christ as "the way, the truth and the life" (John 14:6) that the Church ceaselessly preaches—and indeed is bound to preach because in Christ people find "the fullness of religious life." In his assessment of the impact of *Nostra Aetate* in a volume marking its fiftieth anniversary, Paul F. Knitter in "*Nostra Aetate*: A Milestone" identifies such language in *Nostra Aetate* and in other post–Vatican II magisterial statements as a roadblock to dialogue and cooperation.[33] But dialogues and cooperation have indeed flourished.

POSTCONCILIAR ROMAN CATHOLIC STATEMENTS ON ANTI-JUDAISM, ANTISEMITISM, AND SUPERSESSIONISM

Magisterial statements from the papacies of Paul VI, John Paul II, Benedict XVI, and Francis refer frequently to *Nostra Aetate*, thus attesting to the personal commitments these popes have made to seeing its full implementation. Other curial officials, such as Cardinal Walter Kasper, joined their efforts to improve the Church's relationship with Jews and Judaism. A survey of these papal and curial statements and pronouncements shows how dedicated the postconciliar Church has been in its efforts to rectify its past failures in relation to Jews and to set the Church on a new path of reconciliation and dialogue with them.

Guidelines for Implementing *Nostra Aetate*

On December 1, 1974, shortly after the ninth anniversary of the promulgation of *Nostra Aetate*, the Commission for the Catholic Church's Relations with Jews issued "Guidelines and Suggestions for Implementing the Conciliar Declaration *Nostra Aetate*" (no. 4). Its purpose was a practical one: to foster mutual dialogue and collaboration between Catholics and Jews.

The first heading, "Dialogue," frankly admits the failure of dialogue in the past and a recommendation to probe the riches of one's own tradition while respecting the tradition, faith, and religious convictions of the other, in this case Judaism. The guidelines acknowledge the need for Catholics to preach Jesus Christ to the world yet insist that it be done in a way that is not offensive to Jews. They counsel Catholics to understand the difficulties that Jews have with Christianity's notion of an incarnate Word. Regarding the atmosphere of suspicion in past dialogues, the document advises self-examination to see to what extent Christians were responsible. Moreover, it encourages the parties to meet and study together problems arising from the fundamental convictions of Judaism and Christianity.

Under the second heading, "Liturgy," the document advises that Catholics and Jews strive to understand the links between Christian liturgy and Jewish liturgy, being cognizant of the common elements of both (such as formulas, feasts, rites, and so forth) that derive from the shared biblical traditions. To that end, one guideline stresses the integrity of the Hebrew Bible and the fact that it is neither replaced nor canceled by the New Testament. When addressing the Old and the New Testaments, the continuity between each should be emphasized without opposing the Jewish covenant or minimizing faith elements that originated with the New Testament. Likewise, the guidelines counsel that preaching on biblical texts ought not to distort their meaning, thereby placing Jews in an unfavorable light. Regarding the translations of liturgical texts, care should be taken to eliminate prejudicial language. Here the guidelines acknowledge the supersessionist typological and allegorical interpretation of the Old Testament witnessed in Christian authors already surveyed in the last chapter. They are also aware of the unfortunate translation of the prayer for the conversion of Jews in the Good Friday liturgy discussed earlier.

Under the third heading, "Teaching and Education," the document identifies serious research and study by competent scholars as the beginning of dialogue. Again, stressing the practical nature of these guidelines, a series of facts should be recalled: The Old Testament must not be opposed to the New Testament as though the former witnessed only to justice, fear, and legalism devoid of the love of God. In other words, Marcionism and its vestiges should be rejected. The facts to be remembered are:

1. Jesus, his apostles, and his disciples were Jewish. His Bible was the Old Testament out of which he taught using methods employed by Jewish teachers in his day.
2. The death of Christ should not be blamed on all Jews of his day or on Jews of today (*Nostra Aetate* 4).
3. The history of Judaism did not end with the destruction of Jerusalem. Rather, Jewish traditions continued to be developed, an important reminder that Christianity did not supersede Judaism.
4. Citing *Nostra Aetate* 4 again, the guidelines refer to the prophets and Paul concerning how the Church awaits the day when all peoples will address the Lord and serve him with one arm (Zeph 3:9).
5. Special attention should be given to the preparation of catechisms, religious textbooks, history books, and mass media presentations.

The document also encourages research into the problems bearing on Judaism and Jewish-Christian relations in the areas of exegesis, theology, history, and sociology. It promotes collaboration between Catholic institutions of higher education and similar Christian institutions as they seek solutions to problems in Christian-Jewish relations. Finally, it encourages Catholic colleges and universities to establish chairs of Jewish Studies in consultation with Jewish scholars.

Under the fourth heading, "Joint Social Action," Christians and Jews are encouraged to collaborate willingly in works of social justice and peace on every level—local, national, and international. These guidelines take mutual dialogue and collaboration between Catholics and Jews seriously. They are grounded in the teachings of *Nostra Aetate*, and they recognize not only the need for dialogue but also the long-standing difficulties and problems in such collaboration. This document is not naïve about the long road ahead for successful and satisfactory dialogue between Christians and Jews. And yet it expresses the optimism of the Second Vatican Council and the hope for the full realization of the goals of *Nostra Aetate*.

The Pontifical Biblical Commission

The Pontifical Biblical Commission issued another nonmagisterial, nondoctrinal document, "The Jewish People and Their Sacred Scriptures in the Christian Bible," in 2001.[34] The commission was cognizant of the efforts made in Jewish-Catholic dialogue since Vatican II and wished to make its own contribution to informing that dialogue from the sphere of its expertise, Scripture. The document comprises three chapters and a conclusion that explore the relation of the Old Testament and the New, with a special eye on sticking points in Jewish-Christian relations since the second century CE. The commission gives an overview of its task in the Introduction, which precedes the three main chapters:

> The first chapter lays the foundations by demonstrating that the New Testament recognizes the authority of the Old Testament as divine revelation and that the New Testament cannot be properly understood apart from the Old Testament and the Jewish tradition which transmits it. The second chapter then examines analytically how the writings of the New Testament appropriate the rich content of the Old Testament by developing its

> basic themes in the light of Jesus Christ. Finally, the third chapter reviews the various attitudes which the New Testament writings express regarding the Jews, following, in this respect, the example of the Old Testament itself. (Intro. 1)

Although the commission's document does not use the word *supersessionism*, it does refer to "substitution," eschewing that concept in its description of the relationship of the Church to Israel, while also affirming that Israel's covenant with God has not been revoked. The point is clear:

> The New Testament takes for granted that the election of Israel, the people of the covenant, is irrevocable: it preserves intact its prerogatives (Rm 9:4) and its priority status in history, in the offer of salvation (Ac 13:23) and in the Word of God (13:46)....Far from being a substitution for Israel, the Church is in solidarity with it. (ch. 3, 65c)

Cardinal Walter Kasper

On December 6, 2004, Cardinal Walter Kasper delivered a major address entitled "The Relationship of the Old and the New Covenant as One of the Central Issues in Jewish-Christian Dialogue," at the Centre for the Study of Jewish-Christian Relations in Cambridge, England. At the time, Cardinal Kasper was president of the Pontifical Council for Promoting Christian Unity. He took up the question of the covenant in Jewish-Christian relations and also spoke directly about the problem of supersessionism. He opposed any view held by Christians, that denies the status of Jews as God's chosen people. In so doing, they have wrongly claimed that the old covenant simply prefigured the new covenant. The result was the claim that the Jewish people lost the old covenant, which had now been transferred to Christians.

Cardinal Kasper went on to address the concrete and practical problems resulting from the *substitution theory* (supersessionism). He said,

> This substitution theory has been influential within the Christian tradition. The old covenant was seen as merely prefiguring and preparing the way for the new covenant, it was denied any significance on its own account, let alone any continuing relevance much less a remaining balance of its promise projected into the future. (§3)[35]

He affirmed in no uncertain terms that the old covenant is guaranteed by God's unconditional faithfulness. Consequently, because the old covenant was never revoked (Rom 11:29), the idea of supersessionism has a faulty foundation. The old covenant remains valid and has lasting significance. In support of that fact, Kasper referred to *Nostra Aetate*: "In this declaration the Church expressed regret for every form of anti-Semitism, it affirmed its Jewish roots and, with reference to the Epistle to the Romans, the continued validity of God's covenant with Israel"(§4). Kasper also incorporated Pope John Paul II's repeatedly used term, the "unabrogated covenant," arguing that this opened the door to a redefined relationship between the Church and Judaism.[36] In the footnotes to the address, Kasper mentioned several other members of the hierarchy and scholars who have adopted the "unabrogated covenant" in their discussions of Catholic-Jewish relations after Vatican II, concluding:

> Thus "*Nostra Aetate*" opened a new chapter in the predominantly dark history between Jews and Christians. It represents a new beginning which has in the meantime found resonance in many declarations and official statements at Bishops' Conferences, Synods and Ecclesial Commissions. In the meantime the term "unabrogated covenant" has become the starting point of a renewed theology of Judaism within both Catholic and Protestant theology. In place of treatises "*Contra Judaeis*" [Against Jews] we now find treatises "*De Judaeis*" [About Jews] or "*Pro Judaeis*" [For Jews]. For more recent theology Judaism is not only sociologically but also theologically a current entity. God's covenant with his people has not

> been overtaken and replaced by the new covenant. God has not abrogated his covenant with this people; he has not rejected or forgotten his people. God is still inclined towards these his people in love and faithfulness, in mercy, judgment and forgiveness; he is with them and among them in the difficult hours and times of their history above all. As a member of his people, each Jew continues to stand beneath the promise. (§4)[37]

The import of Cardinal Kasper's remarks cannot be underestimated. His position is unequivocal, and it signals the fact that in official circles the Church explicitly disavows and condemns supersessionism. He recognizes supersessionism as what it always was: a theology driven by religious supremacy that promotes anti-Judaism and antisemitism, and therefore a theology that is not only not viable but also to be rejected. Roman Catholicism and other forms of Christianity have not replaced Judaism. Cardinal Kasper's explicit rejection of supersessionism proved to be a weighty advancement in enabling genuine dialogue and collaboration between Christian and Jews.

Multiple Dialogues

On December 10, 2015, the Commission of the Holy See for Religious Relations issued a theological reflection on the fiftieth anniversary of the promulgation of *Nostra Aetate* entitled "'The Gifts and the Calling of God Are Irrevocable' (Rom 11:29): A Reflection on Theological Questions Pertaining to Catholic-Jewish Relations on the Occasion of the 50th Anniversary of *Nostra Aetate* (No. 4)."[38] Its purpose was to survey the achievements of the Jewish-Catholic dialogue over the previous fifty years and to provide further impetus for that dialogue going forward. Technically speaking, it is not a magisterial document or doctrinal teaching of the Catholic Church. Rather, it is a reflection on the theological questions that have developed regarding the relations of Catholics and Jews since the Second Vatican Council. It was meant to strengthen and intensify the theological dimensions of Jewish-Catholic dialogue.

"The Gifts and Calling of God Are Irrevocable" refers to the Pontifical Biblical Commission's document "The Jewish People and Their Sacred Scriptures in the Christian Bible" as the most significant exegetical document of the Jewish-Catholic dialogue and a treasure trove of the common issues based in Scripture that the dialogue has had to engage. It highlights how the commission's document demonstrates that the Jewish Scriptures are a fundamental component of the Christian Bible and discusses the fundamental scriptural themes of Judaism in its relationship to Christianity. It also praises the portrayal of Jews in the New Testament in detail.[39]

Philip Cunningham, professor of theology and director of the Institute for Jewish-Catholic Relations at Saint Joseph's University in Philadelphia, has published an excellent annotated version of this theological reflection that provides a comprehensive collection of sources that have informed the Jewish-Catholic dialogue since 1965. His article, "The Sources behind 'The Gifts and the Calling of God Are Irrevocable' (Rom 11:29): A Reflection on Theological Questions Pertaining to Catholic-Jewish Relations on the Occasion of the 50th Anniversary of *Nostra Aetate* (4)," is invaluable for understanding the progress that has been made in this dialogue.[40]

Papal Statements and Personal Engagement

The postconciliar popes have also been personally involved in promoting better relationships between the Church and the Jews, and this matters greatly. Since the time of Pope John XXIII, who took the first giant leap forward, Pope Paul VI and the popes of the postconciliar era have been actively engaged in promoting mutual Jewish-Christian dialogue. Their efforts have taken the forms of documents, addresses, speeches, and statements, often further explicating the work of the council in this regard. They led by example in improving the relationship between Catholics and Jews.

On January 10, 1975, Pope Paul VI addressed the Liaison Committee between the Catholic Church and World Judaism at its fourth annual meeting in Rome. This gathering took place shortly after the publication of "Guidelines and Suggestions for Implementing the Conciliar Declaration *Nostra Aetate*" (4). As we have just seen, one of the recommendations of those guidelines was academic collaboration between Catholics and Jews. In his address, Pope Paul referred to the reliance of Thomas Aquinas on the writings of Moshe ben Maimon, better known as Maimonides. Aquinas relied on Maimonides for explanations of the Mosaic Law and the precepts of Judaism. The acknowledgement of Aquinas's exemplary use of Maimonides's thought prompted the pope to refer to the invitation that *Nostra Aetate* encouraged for true dialogue between Judaism and Roman Catholicism. Pope Paul also reaffirmed the Church's rejection of every form of antisemitism and urged all Catholics "to learn by what essential traits the Jews define themselves in the light of their own religious experience."[41] In other words, Catholics should learn about Judaism from Jews themselves to inform their understanding of Judaism as accurately as they can.

The three most recent popes have gone out of their way to signal and embody the importance of the relationship of the Catholic Church and the Jewish people. John Paul II, Benedict XVI, and Francis have all visited the site of the Nazi concentration camp at Auschwitz-Birkenau, where they prayed for the victims of the Shoah and met with Jewish leaders. All three visited the main synagogue in Rome, and all three also visited Israel. Cunningham's summary, referred to above, will suffice to show how important these more personal moments are in promoting dialogue.

> 8. Texts and documents, as important as they are, cannot replace personal encounters and face-to-face dialogues. While under Blessed Pope Paul VI the first steps in Jewish-Catholic dialogue were undertaken, Saint Pope John Paul II succeeded in fostering and deepening this dialogue through compelling gestures towards the Jewish people. He was the first pope to visit the former concentration camp of Auschwitz-Birkenau to pray for the victims of the Shoah, and he visited the Roman Synagogue to express his solidarity with the Jewish community. In the context of an historical pilgrimage to the Holy Land, he was also a guest of the state of Israel

where he participated in interreligious encounters, paid a visit to both Chief Rabbis and prayed at the Western Wall. Again and again, he met with Jewish groups, whether in the Vatican or during his numerous apostolic journeys. So too Benedict XVI, even before his election to the papacy, engaged in Jewish-Catholic dialogue by offering in a series of lectures important theological reflections on the relationship between the Old and the New Covenant, and the Synagogue and the Church. Following his election and in the footsteps of Saint Pope John Paul II he fostered this dialogue in his own way by reinforcing the same gestures and giving expression to his esteem for Judaism through the power of his words. As Archbishop of Buenos Aires, Cardinal Jorge Mario Bergoglio was greatly committed to fostering Jewish-Catholic dialogue and had many friends among the Jews of Argentina. Now as Pope he continues, at the international level, to intensify dialogue with Judaism through many friendly encounters. One of his first such encounters was in May 2014 in Israel, where he met with the two Chief Rabbis, visited the Western Wall, and prayed for the victims of the Shoah in Yad Vashem.[42]

Benedict XVI (2005–2013) and the Good Friday Prayer

There have been some setbacks, however. A bump in the road occurred in July 2007, when Pope Benedict XVI issued his *motu proprio*, *Summorum Pontificum*, which restored the Tridentine Latin Mass under a rubric never before used in the Catholic Church, "the extraordinary form." Regarding the Good Friday prayer for the conversion of the Jews, Benedict reissued the language of the 1962 missal, repeating the language of the veil, blindness, darkness, and the petition for conversion. When Jewish and Catholic leaders pushed back against it, Benedict issued yet another revision:

> Let us pray for the Jews. May the Lord Our God enlighten their hearts so that they may acknowledge Jesus Christ, the savior of all men. Almighty and everlasting God, you who want all men to be saved and to reach the awareness of the truth, graciously grant that, with the fullness of peoples entering into your church, all Israel may be saved.[43]

Pope Benedict's undoing of the revised prayer of the Paul VI missal was met with challenges and reservations. As John R. Donahue commented, it was not clear why the 1970 version of the prayer could not have been retained.[44] Consequently, Benedict suggested that anti-Judaism, antisemitism, and supersessionism were so deeply embedded in Roman Catholicism that they were inescapable. The fact that Pope Benedict reissued the original 1962 Roman Missal translation seemed to have been driven more by his preference for the supremacy of Christ regarding the salvation of humanity than by concern for offending Jews. That desire, however, did not prevent the negative consequences that it caused.

Not only did Pope Benedict restore the 1962 version of the Tridentine Mass, but he also allowed the pre–Vatican II Roman Breviary, the prayer of the Church, to be used again. Rita Ferrone in "Anti-Jewish Elements" has shown that the patristic readings for Matins (the early morning prayer) in Lent, Passiontide, and Holy Week portrayed "the Jews as faithless, sinful, greedy, and blood thirsty people."[45] Moreover, Donahue notes that in the pre–Vatican II Mass only 1 percent of the Scripture readings were taken from the Old Testament.[46] Lack of familiarity with the story of Israel and its worship life is another form of removing Jewish traditions from the life of the Church.

CONCLUSION

The Church has come a long way from the rise of supersessionism in the second century CE to the most recent efforts to correct the errors of supersessionism and to deter its promotion in the life of the Church. It is truly remarkable to see how much progress has been made in the relations between Catholics and Jews, especially since 1965. It is also refreshing to see that both sides in dialogue and collaboration acknowledge that there is still very much to do. The process is on a firm footing and will continue as Jews and Catholics learn more and more about how much they have in common and how different they are from each other. Mutual respect has done much to enhance the dialogue.

CONCLUSION

I have had several goals for writing this book. Aware that many people do not know what supersessionism is, I wanted to introduce them to the problem of supersessionism, hoping to heighten their own awareness of the centuries-long problem it has created for the relationship between Christians and Jews. I also wanted to show that although Christians created this problem, supersessionism is not intrinsic to Christianity but is a distortion of it. Whereas some scholars have identified what they see as incipient supersessionism in certain New Testament texts, I wanted to free those texts from the burden of supersessionist interpretation that resulted from the allegorical method of interpreting Scripture. As a remedy to that way of reading Scripture I offered the historical-critical method of biblical interpretation, which the Catholic Church accepted in the mid-twentieth century.

My intention in calling attention to the relationship between Catholics and Jews in the second half of the twentieth century, the post-Shoah era, was to show how gradual healing has emerged through the efforts and agency of Jews and Catholics whose concerns were finally heard by a newly elected Pope John XXIII. He enthusiastically welcomed the opportunity to right the wrongs of the past. The promulgation of *Nostra Aetate* at the Second Vatican Council in 1965 marked the beginning of a hopeful reversal of the antipathy of Christians to Jews. My objective in focusing on the Roman Catholic Church's condemnation of anti-Judaism, antisemitism, and supersessionism was to underscore how *Nostra Aetate* opened the door to further initiatives for reconciliation, mutual dialogue, and collaboration between Christians and Jews. As a result, Jews and Christians now have opportunities for honestly listening to one another, becoming friends with one another, and seriously trying to find ways to reconcile their differences while maintaining the integrity of what they hold as most sacred. Thus, I wanted to stress that the possibility for healing and friendship between Christians and Jews is one solution to the problem of supersessionism—a goal equally as important as the others I had for this book.

HOPE FOR THE FUTURE

In closing, I want to call attention to some hopeful prospects for the future of Jewish-Christian relations. One is an ongoing research project on Christ and the Jewish people, which is still underway. It explores the Jewishness of Jesus under the title "Christ Jesus the Jew: The Importance of His Jewish Identity for Christians and for Jews Today." This project is cosponsored by The Institute for Jewish-Catholic Relations, the Cardinal Bea Centre for Judaic Studies at the Pontifical Gregorian University in Rome, the Center for Intercultural Theology and the Study of Religions at the Universität Salzburg in Austria, and the Center for Christian-Jewish Learning at Boston College. In September 2022, twenty scholars from ten countries met at St. Joseph's University in Philadelphia with the goal of exploring the significance of the Jewish identity of Jesus for Jews and Christians today, in ways that had not occurred to them previously. These scholars met again in Frankfurt, Germany in February 2024. This time they were hosted by the Universität Salzburg. Boston College welcomed them in September 2024, and the Bea Centre at the Pontifical Gregorian University in Rome in October 2025.[1]

On the fiftieth anniversary of *Nostra Aetate*, Philip Cunningham in *Seeking Shalom: The Journey to Right Relationship between Catholics and Jews*, wrote about a new relationship between Catholics and Jews that is like a *chavruta*, a Hebrew/Aramaic term that means a "learning partner."[2] It was proposed for this purpose by Rabbi Daniel Lehmann, the former president of the Graduate Theological Union at Berkeley. The word can also be translated as "friend." It is a rabbinic method of learning in which the quality of the relationship between students is as important as the object of their study. Cunningham invokes the friendship between Pope Francis and Rabbi Abraham Skorka to illustrate the value of having such a *chavruta*.[3]

Because a formal dialogue does not always produce mutual learning, *chavruta* is an appropriate way to describe what Christians and Jews hope will result from talking and listening to one another. The metaphor connotes mutual learning and teaching in a relationship of trust where hard questions can be engaged for the benefit of both parties. Cunningham lists three principles that apply to the quality of mutuality in a *chavruta* relationship:

1. "The otherness of the Jewish or Christian interlocutor must be cherished."
2. "The nature of any differences needs to be analyzed carefully."
3. "Seeking the Holy One together."[4]

In 2022, Cunningham expanded those principles to ten maxims for mutuality in a book of the same name, *Maxims for Mutuality: Principles for Catholic Theology, Education, and Preaching about Jews and Judaism*.[5]

Adhering to those principles inescapably requires hard work. Such mutuality was not possible in previous generations when Jews and Christians had little or no contact with each other. Yet, given all the efforts made by Christians and Jews since 1965, entering a learning partner relationship promises to build better relationships between Christians and Jews for the future. Cunningham suggests that both Christians and Jews should follow a maxim of rabbinic advice to "find yourself a teacher, make yourself a friend, and judge every person favorably" (Pirke Avot 1:6) to accomplish this meaningful mutuality.[6]

ACKNOWLEDGEMENTS

Cunningham, Philip A. "The Sources behind 'The Gifts and the Calling of God Are Irrevocable' (Rom 11:29): A Reflection on Theological Questions Pertaining to Catholic-Jewish Relations on the Occasion of the 50th Anniversary of *Nostra Aetate* (No. 4)." *Studies in Christian-Jewish Relations* 12 (2017): 1–39. Reproduced courtesy of the author.

Ehrman, Bart D., ed. *The Apostolic Fathers*. 2 vols. Cambridge, MA: Harvard University Press, 2003. Reproduced courtesy of Harvard University Press.

Irenaeus of Lyons. *Against Heresies*. Translated and annotated by Dominic Unger, OFM Cap. With an introduction and further revisions by Scott Moringiello. Ancient Christian Writers 72. Mahwah, NJ: Newman Press, 2024. Reproduced courtesy of Paulist Press.

Jefford, Clayton N. *The Epistle to Diognetus (with the Fragment of Quadratus): Introduction, Text and Commentary*. Oxford: Oxford University Press, 2013. Reproduced courtesy of Oxford University Press.

John Chrysostom. *Discourses against Judaizing Christians*. Translated by Paul W. Harkins. Fathers of the Church 68. Washington, DC: The Catholic University of America Press, 1977. Reproduced courtesy of The Catholic University of America Press.

Justin Martyr, Saint. *Dialogue with Trypho*. Selections from the Fathers of the Church 3. Translated by Thomas B. Falls. Revised and with a New Introduction by Thomas P. Halton. Edited by Michael Slusser. Washington, DC: The Catholic University of America Press, 2003. Reproduced courtesy of the Catholic University of America Press.

Melito of Sardis. *On Pascha: with the Fragments of Melito and Other Material Related to the Quartodecimans*. Translated, introduced, and annotated by Alistair Stewart-Sykes. Crestwood, NY: St. Vladimir's Seminary Press, 2001. Reproduced courtesy of St. Vladimir's Seminary Press.

NOTES

CHAPTER 1

1. J. Carleton Paget, "Jewish Christianity," in *The Cambridge History of Judaism* (Cambridge: Cambridge University Press, 1999), 731–42.

2. Paget, "Jewish Christianity," 740.

3. Paget, "Jewish Christianity," 734, 742.

4. Brendan Byrne, SJ, *Lifting the Burden: Reading Matthew's Gospel in the Church Today* (Collegeville, MN: Liturgical Press, 2004), 2.

5. J. A. Simpson and E. S. C Weiner, eds, *The Oxford English Dictionary*, 2nd ed. (New York: Oxford University Press, 1989).

6. See R. Kendall Soulen, *The God of Israel and Christian Theology* (Minneapolis: Fortress, 2009), 29–31.

7. See Lloyd Kim, *Polemic in the Book of Hebrews: Anti-Semitism, Anti-Judaism, Supersessionism?*, Princeton Theological Monographs 34 (Eugene, OR: Pickwick, 2006), 2–7.

8. Ivan G. Marcus, *How the West Became Antisemitic: Jews and the Formation of Europe, 800–1500* (Princeton, NJ: Princeton University Press, 2024), 190.

9. Marcus, *How the West Became Antisemitic*, 192.

10. Marcus, *How the West Became Antisemitic*, 189.

11. See Marcus, *How the West Became Antisemitic*, 196–98.

12. See Marcus, *How the West Became Antisemitic*, 18, 196–99.

13. Marcus, *How the West Became Antisemitic*, 18, 198. Emphasis added.

14. Marcus, *How the West Became Antisemitic*, 18.

15. Marcus, *How the West Became Antisemitic*, 18.

16. See Marcus, *How the West Became Antisemitic*, 18.

17. See Marcus, *How the West Became Antisemitic*, 196.

18. See Marcus, *How the West Became Antisemitic*, 4, 198.

19. Marcus, *How the West Became Antisemitic*, 6–9.

20. Reidar Hvalvik, *The Struggle for Scripture and Covenant: The Purpose of the Epistle of Barnabas and Jewish-Christian Competition in the Second Century*, Wissenschaftliche Untersuchungen zum Neuen Testament, Series 2, 82 (Tübingen: Mohr Siebeck, 1996), 22.

CHAPTER 2

1. Krister Stendahl, "The Apostle Paul and the Introspective Conscience of the West," *The Harvard Theological Review* 56 (1963): 204–5.

2. Matthew Thiessen, *A Jewish Paul: The Messiah's Herald to the Gentiles* (Grand Rapids, MI: Baker Academic, 2023), 59–60.

3. See Thiessen, *A Jewish Paul*, 62–65.

4. See Thiessen, *A Jewish Paul*, 91–92.

5. See Thiessen, *A Jewish Paul*, 93.

6. See Thiessen, *A Jewish Paul*, 30.

7. See Thiessen, *A Jewish Paul*, 104–5.

8. Daniel J. Harrington, SJ, *The Gospel of Matthew*, Sacra Pagina 1 (Collegeville, MN: Liturgical Press, 1991), 10–16.

9. See Harrington, *Gospel of Matthew*, 12.

10. See Harrington, *Gospel of Matthew*, 12–14.

11. See Harrington, *Gospel of Matthew*, 12.

12. See Harrington, *Gospel of Matthew*, 14.

13. See Harrington, *Gospel of Matthew*, 17.

14. See Harrington, *Gospel of Matthew*, 17.

15. See Harrington, *Gospel of Matthew*, 83–84.

16. See Harrington, *Gospel of Matthew*, 20–22.

17. J. Andrew Overman, *Matthew's Gospel and Formative Judaism* (Minneapolis: Fortress Press, 1990), 19–23.

18. Daniel J. Harrington, SJ, "The Gradual Emergence of the Church and the Parting of the Ways," in *Christ Jesus and the Jewish People Today: New Explorations of Theological Relationships*, ed. Philip A. Cunningham, et al. (Grand Rapids, MI: Eerdmans, 2011), 99.

19. Harrington, *Gospel of Matthew*, 390–92.

20. See Harrington, *Gospel of Matthew*, 20–22.

21. See Harrington, "The Gradual Emergence of the Church," 100.

22. J. Louis Martyn, *History and Theology in the Fourth Gospel.* 2nd ed. (Nashville: Abingdon, 1979).

23. Raymond E. Brown, *The Community of the Beloved Disciple* (New York: Paulist Press, 1979).

24. Jouette Bassler, "The Galileans: A Neglected Factor in Johannine Community Research," *The Catholic Biblical Quarterly* 43 (1981): 243–52.

25. Bassler, "The Galileans," 243–46.

26. See Bassler, "The Galileans," 252.

27. Bassler, "The Galileans," 253.

28. Bassler, "The Galileans," 254–56.

29. See Bassler, "The Galileans," 255, 257.

30. Paul Anderson, *The Riddles of the Fourth Gospel: An Introduction to John* (Minneapolis: Fortress Press, 2011), 190–93.

31. Anderson, *The Riddles of the Fourth Gospel*, 38–39.

32. Norman P. Tanner, *Decrees of the Ecumenical Councils*, 2 vols. (Washington, DC: Georgetown University Press, 1990), 732–33.

33. See Alan C. Mitchell, "The Reception of Hebrews in the Roman Catholic Tradition at the Council of Trent," in *The Oxford Handbook of Hebrews and The Catholic Tradition*, ed. Patrick Gray (Oxford: Oxford University Press, 2024), 406–7.

34. Philip Church, "Hebrews and the Question of Supersessionism," in *The Oxford Handbook of Hebrews and the Catholic Tradition*, ed. Patrick Gray (Oxford: Oxford University Press, 2024), 176.

35. See Alan C. Mitchell, "'A Sacrifice of Praise': Does Hebrews Promote Supersessionism?," in *Reading the Epistle to the Hebrews*, ed. Eric Farrel Mason and Kevin B McCruden (Atlanta: Society of Biblical Literature, 2011), 251–67.

36. See Alan C. Mitchell, *Hebrews*, Sacra Pagina 13 (Collegeville, MN: Liturgical Press, 2009), 1–34; Christine R. Trotter, *Hellenistic Jews and Consolatory Rhetoric: 2 Maccabees, Wisdom of Solomon, 1 Thessalonians, and Hebrews*, Wissenschaftliche Untersuchungen zum Neuen Testament, Series 2, 600 (Tübingen: Mohr Siebeck, 2023), 233–79.

37. See Mitchell, "A Sacrifice of Praise," 252–57.

38. See Alan C. Mitchell, "We Have Such a High Priest": Encouragement in Hebrews," in *The Figure of Jesus in History and*

Theology: Essays in Honor of John Meier, ed. Vincent T. M. Skemp and Kelley Coblentz Bautch (Washington, DC: The Catholic Biblical Association of America, 2020), 252–57.

39. See Jesper Svartvik, "Reading the Epistle to the Hebrews without Presupposing Supersessionism," in Cunningham et al., *Christ Jesus and the Jewish People Today*, 81–88.

40. Walter Kasper, "The Relationship of the Old and the New Covenant as One of the Central Issues in Jewish-Christian Dialogue," delivered at the Centre for the Study of Jewish-Christian Relations, Cambridge, UK, December 6, 2004, https://ccjr.us/dialogika-resources/documents-and-statements/roman-catholic/kasper/kasper04dec6-1.

CHAPTER 3

1. See Clayton N. Jefford, *The Epistle to Diognetus (with the Fragment of Quadratus): Introduction, Text and Commentary* (Oxford: Oxford University Press, 2013), 19. Hereinafter referred to as *Diognetus* in the text.

2. See Jefford, *Epistle to Diognetus*, 209–10.

3. Justin, Philosopher and Martyr, *Apologies*, ed. with commentary Denis Minns and Paul Parvis, Oxford Early Christian Texts (Oxford: Oxford University Press, 2009), 32–41. Referred to in the text as *First Apology*. There are two apologies in this book; the first is referred to as Justin's *Apology on Behalf of Christians*, the other is *The Second Apology*. I changed "Apologies" to "First Apology," which is how it is commonly referred to.

4. See Oskar Skarsaune, *The Proof from Prophecy: A Study in Justin Martyr's Proof-Text Tradition: Text-Type, Provenance, Theological Profile* (Leiden: Brill, 1980), 409–24.

5. See Timothy J. Horner, *"Listening to Trypho": Justin Martyr's Dialogue Reconsidered* (Leuven: Peeters, 2001), 25.

6. See Horner, *Listening to Trypho*, 26–29.

7. See Claudia Setzer, *Jewish Responses to Early Christians: History and Polemics, 30–150 C.E.* (Minneapolis: Fortress Press, 1994), 129.

8. See Horner, *Listening to Trypho*, 16–19.

9. Justin Martyr, *Dialogue with Trypho*, selections from the Fathers of the Church 3, trans. Thomas B. Falls, rev. with a new introduction by Thomas P. Halton, ed. Michael Slusser (Washington, DC: Catholic University of America Press, 2003). Referred to in the text as *Dialogue*. I changed this because "Trypho" suggests that he is the only one speaking. *Dialogue* reflects the nature of the work.

10. See Horner, *Listening to Trypho*, 19–32.

11. See Justin Martyr, *Dialogue* 23.4, 34.1; 43.1; 67.9–10; 122.5–6; and 123.1.

12. See Joseph A. Fitzmyer, SJ, *The One Who Is to Come* (Grand Rapids, MI: Eerdmans, 2007), 59.

13. See Daniel Boyarin, "Justin Martyr Invents Judaism," *Church History* (2001): 458.

14. See Justin Martyr, *First Apology* 35.1–9; 36.1–3; 37.1–38.8; 49.5; 63.1–10.

15. See Justin Martyr, *First Apology* 35.1–9; 36.1–3; 37.1–38.8; 49.5; 63.1–10.

16. See Adolf von Harnack, *Marcion: Das Evangelium vom fremden Gott* (Leipzig: J. C. Hinrichs'sche Buchhandlung, 1924). English trans. *Marcion: The Gospel of the Alien God*, trans. John E. Steely and Lyle D. Bierma (Durham, NC: Labyrinth Press, 1990), 15–20.

17. See Irenaeus of Lyons, *Against the Heresies*, trans. and annotated Dominic Unger, OFM Cap, with an introduction and further revisions by Scott Moringiello, Ancient Christian Writers 72 (Mahwah, NJ: Newman Press, 2024), 4.1.1–2; 2.1–7; 33:2. Referred to in the text as Irenaeus.

18. See Tertullian, *Adversus Marcionem*, trans. Ernest Evans (Oxford: Clarendon Press, 1972), 643–46.

19. Melito of Sardis, *On Pascha: with the Fragments of Melito and Other Material Related to the Quartodecimans*, trans., introduced, and annotated Alistair Stewart-Sykes (Crestwood, NY: St. Vladimir's Seminary Press, 2001), 1–5. Referred to in the text as Melito.

20. See Melito, *On Pascha*, 82; Irenaeus, *Against Heresies* 4. 9.1–2.

21. Wayne A. Meeks and Robert Wilken, *Jews and Christians in the First Four Centuries of the Common Era* (Missoula, MT: Scholars Press, 1978), 25–27.

22. See Meeks and Wilken, *Jews and Christians*, 29–30.

23. Marcel Simon, *Verus Israel: A Study of the Relations between Christians and Jews in the Roman Empire (135–425)* (Oxford: Oxford University Press, 1986), 217.

24. John Chrysostom, *Discourses against Judaizing Christians*, Fathers of the Church 68, trans. Paul W. Harkins (Washington, DC: Catholic University of America Press, 1977). Referred to in the text as *Discourses*.

25. A. Lukyn Williams, *Adversus Judaeos: A Bird's-Eye View of Christian Apologetic until the Renaissance* (Cambridge: Cambridge University Press, 1935).

26. See Williams, *Adversus Judaeos*, 417.

27. John T. Pawlikowski, "Religion as Hatred: Antisemitism as a Case Study," *Journal of Hate Studies* 3 (2003–2004): 37–48.

28. John T. Pawlikowski, "Has Antisemitism Been Uprooted from Christianity? A Catholic Response," *Antisemitism Studies* 6 (2022): 257.

29. See Meeks and Wilken, *Jews and Christians*, 34.

CHAPTER 4

1. John W. O'Malley, *What Happened at Vatican II* (Cambridge, MA: Harvard University Press), 54.

2. O'Malley, *What Happened at Vatican II*, 68.

3. O'Malley, *What Happened at Vatican II*, 69.

4. John M. Oesterreicher, "*Pro Perfidis Judaeis*," *Theological Studies* 8 (1947): 80.

5. See Gregory Baum, *The Jews and the Gospel: A Re-examination of the New Testament* (Westminster, MD: The Newman Press, 1961), 9–10.

6. Emma Fattorini, *Hitler, Mussolini, and the Vatican: Pope Pius XI and the Speech That Was Never Made* (Cambridge: Polity Press, 2011), 109.

7. Fattorini, *Hitler, Mussolini and the Vatican*, 110.

8. See Egal Feldman, *Catholics and Jews in Twentieth Century America* (Chicago: University of Illinois Press, 2001), 54.

9. Pius XI. *Mit brennender Sorge* 21. https://www.vatican.va/content/pius-xi/en/encyclicals/documents/hf_p-xi_enc_14031937_mit-brennender-sorge.html.

10. See Fattorini, *Hitler, Mussolini, and the Vatican*, 152–57.

11. In 1995, Georges Passelecq and Bernard Suchecky published *L'Encyclique cachée de Pie XI: une occasion manquée de l'Eglise face à l'antisémitisme* (Paris: Editions La Découverte, 1995). Two years later an English translation appeared, *The Hidden Encyclical of Pius XI* (New York: Harcourt Brace, 1997). Passelecq and Suchecky tell the story of the discovery by Thomas Breslin, SJ, of what appeared to be drafts of the encyclical of Pius XI among the papers of John LaFarge, SJ. Apparently, LaFarge, Gundlach, and Desbuqois composed the drafts of the encyclical in French, English, and German with one of them entitled *Humani Generis Unitas*, "The Unity of the Human Race." The foreword to the reconstructed encyclical describes it as three fragments drawn from the three drafts that are not identical or complete in their content. In addition, there are questions about whether the drafts themselves represent the thought of Pius XI on racism and antisemitism. Consequently, the value of the reconstructed encyclical as a papal document is unclear. According to the Passelecq and Suchecky, their version of *Humani Generis Unitas* remains hypothetical (60).

12. See Fattorini, *Hitler, Mussolini and the Vatican*, 155.

13. See Fattorini, *Hitler, Mussolini, and the Vatican*, 161.

14. See John Connelly, *From Enemy to Brother: The Revolution in Catholic Teaching on the Jews, 1933–1965* (Cambridge, MA: Harvard University Press, 2012), 1–146.

15. David I. Kertzer and Roberto Benedetti, "In the Wake of the Holocaust: Massimo Vitale, Pius XII, and the Battle over the Good Friday Prayer for the 'Perfidious Jews,'" *Studies in Christian-Jewish Relations* 18, no. 1 (2023): 1–24.

16. See Kertzer and Benedetti, "In the Wake of the Holocaust," 4.

17. See Kertzer and Benedetti, "In the Wake of the Holocaust," 7–11.

18. Kertzer and Benedetti, "In the Wake of the Holocaust," 11–21.

19. O'Malley, *What Happened at Vatican II*, 84.

20. O'Malley, *What Happened at Vatican II*, 83.

21. See Kertzer and Benedetti, "In the Wake of the Holocaust," 22–23.

22. Quoted in Rita Ferrone, "Anti-Jewish Elements in the Extraordinary Form," *Worship* 84 (2010): 499.

23. https://ccjr.us/dialogika-resources/documents-and-statements/roman-catholic/pope-benedict-xvi/b1608feb5.

24. https://www.vatican.va/archive/hist_councils/ii_vatican_council/documents/vat-ii_decl_19651207_dignitatis-humanae_en.html.

25. https://www.vatican.va/archive/hist_councils/ii_vatican_council/documents/vat-ii_const_19641121_lumen-gentium_en.html.

26. O'Malley, *What Happened at Vatican II*, 6–7.

27. John Borelli, "*Nostra Aetate*: Origin, History, and Vatican II Context," in *The Future of Interreligious Dialogue: A Multireligious Conversation on* Nostra Aetate, ed. Charles L. Cohen, Paul F. Knitter, and Ulrich Rosenhagen (Maryknoll, NY: Orbis Books, 2017), 23.

28. See Borelli, "*Nostra Aetate*," 23–28.

29. Leo Lefebure, *True and Holy* (Maryknoll, NY: Orbis Books, 2014), 92.

30. https://www.vatican.va/archive/hist_councils/ii_vatican_council/documents/vat-ii_decl_19651028_nostra-aetate_en.html.

31. See Borelli, "*Nostra Aetate*," 23.

32. David Hollenbach, *Human Rights in a Divided World: Catholicism as a Living Tradition* (Washington, DC: Georgetown University Press, 2024), 5.

33. See Paul F. Knitter, "*Nostra Aetate*: A Milestone in the History of Religions from Competition to Cooperation," in Cohen, Knitter, and Rosenhagen, *The Future of Interreligious Dialogue*, 50–58.

34. Available at https://www.vatican.va/roman_curia/congregations/cfaith/pcb_documents/rc_con_cfaith_doc_20020212_popolo-ebraico_en.html.

35. Walter Kasper, "The Relationship of the Old and the New Covenant as One of the Central Issues in Jewish-Christian Dialogue," https://ccjr.us/dialogika-resources/documents-and-statements/roman-catholic/kasper/kasper04dec6-1.

36. See David M. Gordis, "John Paul II and the Jews," and Byron L. Sherwin, "John Paul II's Catholic Theology of Judaism," in *John Paul II and Interreligious Dialogue*, ed. Byron L. Sherwin and Harold Kasimov (Maryknoll, NY: Orbis Books, 1999), 125–38; 138–66.

37. Kasper, "The Relationship of the Old and the New Covenant," §4.

38. http://www.christianunity.va/content/unitacristiani/en/commissione-per-i-rapporti-religiosi-con-l-ebraismo/commissione-per-i-rapporti-religiosi-con-l-ebraismo-crre/documenti-della-commissione/en.html.

39. "The Gifts and Calling of God Are Irrevocable," 7.

40. *Studies in Christian and Jewish Relations* 12 (2017): 1–39.

41. https://www.vatican.va/content/paul-vi/en/speeches/1975/documents/hf_p-vi_spe_19750110_chiesa-cattolica-ebraismo.html.

42. *Studies in Christian and Jewish Relations* 12 (2017): 1–39.

43. https://ccjr.us/dialogika-resources/documents-and-statements/roman-catholic/pope-benedict-xvi/b1608feb5.

44. See John R. Donahue, "Trouble Ahead? The Future of Jewish Catholic Relations," *Commonweal* 136 (2009): 20.

45. Ferrone, "Anti-Jewish Elements," 500–503.

46. See Donahue, "Trouble Ahead?" 21.

CONCLUSION

1. https://www.sju.edu/IJCR-to-host-CJJ.

2. Philip A. Cunningham, *Seeking Shalom: The Journey to Right Relationship between Catholics and Jews* (Grand Rapids, MI: Eerdmans, 2015), 248–56.

3. Cunningham, *Seeking Shalom*, 248–56.

4. Cunningham, *Seeking Shalom*, 253–55.

5. Philip A. Cunningham, *Maxims for Mutuality: Principles for Catholic Theology, Education, and Preaching about Jews and Judaism* (Mahwah, NJ: Paulist Press, 2022).

6. Cunningham, *Seeking Shalom*, 252–53.

BIBLIOGRAPHY

Anderson, Paul N. *The Riddles of the Fourth Gospel: An Introduction to John*. Minneapolis: Fortress Press, 2011.

Baron, Lori, Jill Hicks-Keeton, and Matthew Thiessen, eds. *The Ways That Often Parted: Essays in Honor of Joel Marcus*. Early Christianity and Its Literature 24. Atlanta: SBL Press, 2018.

Bassler, Jouette M. "The Galileans: A Neglected Factor in Johannine Community Research." *The Catholic Biblical Quarterly* 43 (1981): 243–57.

Baum, Gregory. *Amazing Church: A Catholic Theologian Remembers a Half-Century of Change*. Maryknoll, NY: Orbis Books, 2005.

———. *Is the New Testament Anti-Semitic?* Glen Rock, NJ: Paulist Press, 1965.

———. *The Jews and the Gospel: A Re-examination of the New Testament*. Westminster, MD: The Newman Press, 1961.

Becker, Adam H., and Annette Yoshiko Reed. *The Ways That Never Parted: Jews and Christians in Late Antiquity and the Early Middle Ages*. Texte und Studien zum antiken Judentum 95. Tübingen: Mohr Siebeck, 2003.

Benedict XVI, Pope. *Summorum Pontificum*. 2007. https://www.vatican.va/content/benedict-xvi/en/motu_proprio/documents/hf_ben-xvi_motu-proprio_20070707_summorum-pontificum.html.

Borelli, John. "*Nostra Aetate*: Origin, History, and Vatican II Context." In *The Future of Interreligious Dialogue: A Multireligious Conversation on Nostra Aetate*, edited by Charles L. Cohen, Paul F. Knitter, and Ulrich Rosenhagen, 23–43. Maryknoll, NY: Orbis Books, 2017.

Boyarin, Daniel. "Justin Martyr Invents Judaism." *Church History* (2001): 427–61.

Boys, Mary C., and Sara S. Lee. *Christians and Jews in Dialogue: Learning in the Presence of the Other.* Woodstock, VT: SkyLight Paths Publications, 2006.

Brown, Raymond Edward. *The Community of the Beloved Disciple: The Life, Loves and Hates of an Individual Church in New Testament Times.* New York: Paulist Press, 1979.

Byrne, Brendan, SJ. *Lifting the Burden: Reading Matthew's Gospel in the Church Today.* Collegeville, MN: Liturgical Press, 2004.

Church, Philip. "Hebrews and the Question of Supersessionism." In *The Oxford Handbook of Hebrews and The Catholic Tradition*, edited by Patrick Gray, 157–80. Oxford: Oxford University Press, 2024.

Commission of the Holy See for Religious Relations. "'The Gifts and the Calling of God Are Irrevocable' (Rom 11:29): A Reflection on Theological Questions Pertaining to Catholic-Jewish Relations on the Occasion of the 50th Anniversary of *Nostra Aetate* (No. 4)." https://bit.ly/4eKuEbn.

Commission for the Catholic Church's Relations with Jews. "Guidelines and Suggestions for Implementing the Conciliar Declaration *Nostra Aetate*" (no. 4). https://www.christianunity.va/content/unitacristiani/en/commissione-per-i-rapporti-religiosi-con-l-ebraismo/commissione-per-i-rapporti-religiosi-con-l-ebraismo-crre/documenti-della-commissione/en3.html.

Connelly, John. *From Enemy to Brother: The Revolution in Catholic Teaching on the Jews, 1933–1965.* Cambridge, MA: Harvard University Press, 2012.

Cunningham, Philip A., Joseph Sievers, Mary Boys, Hans Hermann Henrix, and Jesper Svartvik, eds. *Christ Jesus and the Jewish People Today: New Explorations of Theological Interrelationships.* Grand Rapids, MI: Eerdmans, 2011.

———. *Maxims for Mutuality: Principles for Catholic Theology, Education, and Preaching about Jews and Judaism.* Mahwah, NJ: Paulist Press, 2022.

———. *Seeking Shalom: The Journey to Right Relationship between Catholics and Jews.* Grand Rapids, MI: Eerdmans, 2015.

———. *Sharing the Scriptures.* Mahwah, NJ: Paulist Press, 2003.

———. "The Sources behind 'The Gifts and the Calling of God Are Irrevocable' (Rom 11:29): A Reflection on Theological Questions Pertaining to Catholic-Jewish Relations on the Occasion of the 50th Anniversary of *Nostra Aetate* (No. 4)." *Studies in Christian-Jewish Relations* 12 (2017): 1–39.

———. *A Story of Shalom: The Calling of Christians and Jews by a Covenanting God.* New York / Mahwah, NJ: Paulist Press, 2001.

Cunningham, Philip A, Norbert Johannes Hofmann, and Joseph Sievers, eds. *The Catholic Church and the Jewish People: Recent Reflections from Rome.* New York: Fordham University Press, 2007.

"*Dabru Emet:* A Jewish Statement on Christians and Christianity." https://www.ccjr.us/dialogika-resources/documents-and-statements/jewish/dabru-emet.

Donahue, John R. "Trouble Ahead? The Future of Jewish Catholic Relations." *Commonweal* 136 (2009): 19–23.

Donaldson, Terence L. "Supersessionism and Early Christian Self-Definition." *Journal of the Jesus Movement in Its Jewish Setting* 3 (2016): 1–32.

Dunn, James D. G. *The Partings of the Ways: Between Christianity and Judaism and Their Significance for the Character of Christianity.* 2nd ed. London: SCM, 2006.

Ehrman, Bart D., ed. *The Apostolic Fathers.* 2 vols. Cambridge, MA: Harvard University Press, 2003.

Epiphanius of Salamis. *The Panarion of Epiphanius of Salamis*, Book I (Sects. 1–46). Nag Hammadi & Manichean Studies 63. Translated by Frank Williams. Leiden: Brill, 2009.

Eusebius of Caesarea. Ecclesiastical History. Translated by Kirsopp Lake, John Ernest Leonard Oulton, and Hugh Jackson Lawlor. Loeb Classical Library 153. New York: G.P. Putnam's Sons, 1926.

Fattorini, Emma. *Hitler, Mussolini, and the Vatican: Pope Pius XI and the Speech That Was Never Made.* Cambridge: Polity Press, 2011.

Fitzmyer, Joseph A. *The One Who Is to Come.* Grand Rapids, MI: Eerdmans, 2007.

Feldman, Egal. *Catholics and Jews in Twentieth Century America.* Chicago: University of Illinois Press, 2001.

Ferrone, Rita. "Anti-Jewish Elements in the Extraordinary Form." *Worship* 84 (2010): 498–513.

Frerichs, Ernest S., Caroline McCracken-Flesher, and Jacob Neusner, eds. *"To See Ourselves as Others See Us": Christians, Jews, "Others" in Late Antiquity."* Chico, CA: Scholars Press, 1985.

Harnack, Adolf von. *Marcion: Das Evangelium vom fremden Gott.* Leipzig: J.C. Hinrichs'sche Buchhandlung, 1924. English Translation: *Marcion: The Gospel of the Alien God.* Translated by John E. Steely and Lyle D. Bierma. Durham, NC: The Labyrinth Press, 1990.

Harrington, Daniel J. *The Gospel of Matthew.* Sacra Pagina 1. Collegeville, MN: Liturgical Press, 1991.

———. "The Gradual Emergence of the Church and the Parting of the Ways." In *Christ Jesus and the Jewish People Today: New Explorations of Theological Relationships*, edited by Philip A. Cunningham, Joseph Sievers, Mary Boys, Hans Hermann Henrix, and Jesper Svartvik, 92–104. Grand Rapids, MI: Eerdmans, 2011.

Hollenbach, David. *Human Rights in a Divided World: Catholicism as a Living Tradition.* Washington, DC: Georgetown University Press, 2024.

Horner, Timothy J. *"Listening to Trypho": Justin Martyr's Dialogue Reconsidered.* Leuven: Peeters, 2001.

Hvalvik, Reidar. *The Struggle for Scripture and Covenant: The Purpose of the Epistle of Barnabas and Jewish-Christian Competition in the Second Century.* Wissenschaftliche Untersuchungen zum Neuen Testament 2. Series 82. Tübingen: Mohr Siebeck, 1996.

Irenaeus of Lyons. *Against Heresies.* Translated and annotated by Dominic Unger, OFM Cap. With an introduction and further revisions by Scott Moringiello. Ancient Christian Writers 72. Mahwah, NJ: Newman Press, 2024.

Isaac, Jules. *Jésus et Israël.* Paris: Albin Michel, 1948. New edition. Paris: Fasquelle, 1959. English translation: *Jesus and Israel.* New York: Holt, Rinehart and Winston, 1971.

Jefford, Clayton N. *The Epistle to Diognetus (with the Fragment of Quadratus): Introduction, Text and Commentary.* Oxford: Oxford University Press, 2013.

John Chrysostom. *Discourses against Judaizing Christians.* Translated by Paul W. Harkins. The Fathers of the Church 68. Washington, DC: Catholic University of America Press, 1977.

Justin Martyr. *Apologies*. Edited with a commentary on the text by Denis Minns and Paul Parvis. Oxford Early Christian Texts. Oxford: Oxford University Press, 2009.

———. *Dialogue with Trypho*. Selections from the Fathers of the Church. Translated by Thomas B. Falls. Revised and with a new introduction by Thomas P. Halton. Edited by Michael Slusser. Washington, DC: Catholic University of America Press, 2003.

Kasper, Walter. "The Relationship of the Old and the New Covenant as One of the Central Issues in Jewish-Christian Dialogue." https://ccjr.us/dialogika-resources/documents-and-statements/roman-catholic/kasper/kasper04dec6-1.

Kertzer, David I., and Roberto Benedetti. "In the Wake of the Holocaust: Massimo Vitale, Pius XII, and the Battle over the Good Friday Prayer for the 'Perfidious Jews.'" *Studies in Christian-Jewish Relations* 18, no. 1 (2023): 1–24.

Kim, Lloyd. *Polemic in the Book of Hebrews: Anti-Semitism, Anti-Judaism, Supersessionism?* Princeton Theological Monographs 34. Eugene, OR: Pickwick, 2006.

Knitter, Paul F. "*Nostra Aetate*: A Milestone in the History of Religions, from Competition to Cooperation." In *The Future of Interreligious Dialogue: A Multireligious Conversation on Nostra Aetate*, edited by Charles L. Cohen, Paul F. Knitter, and Ulrich Rosenhagen, 50–58. Maryknoll, NY: Orbis Books, 2017.

Lefebure, Leo D. *True and Holy*. Maryknoll, NY: Orbis Books, 2014.

Levine, Amy-Jill. "Supersessionism: Admit and Address Rather than Debate or Deny." *Religions* 13 (2022): 155–67.

Levine, Amy-Jill, and Marc Zvi Brettler, eds. *The Bible with and without Jesus: How Jews and Christians Read the Same Stories Differently*. New York: HarperOne, 2020.

———. *The Jewish Annotated New Testament: New Revised Standard Version Bible Translation*. 2nd ed. Oxford: Oxford University Press, 2017.

Marcus, Ivan G. *How the West Became Antisemitic: Jews and the Formation of Europe, 800–1500*. 1st ed. Princeton, NJ: Princeton University Press, 2024.

Martyn, J. Louis. *History & Theology in the Fourth Gospel*. Nashville: Abingdon, 1979.

Meeks, Wayne A., and Robert Wilken. *Jews and Christians in the First Four Centuries of the Common Era*. Missoula, MT: Scholars Press, 1978.

Melito of Sardis. *On Pascha: with the Fragments of Melito and Other Material Related to the Quartodecimans*. Translated, introduced, and annotated by Alistair Stewart-Sykes. Crestwood, NY: St. Vladimir's Seminary Press, 2001.

Melloni, Alberto. "Nostra Aetate and the Discovery of the Sacrament of Otherness." In *The Catholic Church and the Jewish People: Recent Reflections from Rome*, edited by Philip A. Cunningham, Norbert Johannes Hofmann, and Joseph Sievers, 129–51. New York: Fordham University Press, 2007.

Mitchell, Alan C. "'A Sacrifice of Praise:' Does Hebrews Promote Supersessionism?" In *Reading the Epistle to the Hebrews*, edited by Eric Farrel Mason and Kevin B. McCruden, 251–67. Atlanta: Society of Biblical Literature, 2011.

———. *Hebrews*. Sacra Pagina 13. Collegeville, MN: Liturgical Press, 2009.

———. "The Reception of Hebrews in the Roman Catholic Tradition at the Council of Trent." In *The Oxford Handbook of Hebrews and The Catholic Tradition*, edited by Patrick Gray, 401–12. Oxford: Oxford University Press, 2024.

———. "'We Have Such a High Priest': Encouragement in Hebrews." In *The Figure of Jesus in History and Theology: Essays in Honor of John Meier*, edited by Vincent T. M. Skemp and Kelley Coblentz Bautch, 244–58. Washington, DC: Catholic Biblical Association of America, 2020.

Moore, Nicholas J. *Repetition in Hebrews: Plurality and Singularity in the Letter to the Hebrews, Its Ancient Context, and the Early Church*. Wissenschaftliche Untersuchungen zum Neuen Testament 2. Series 388. Tübingen: Mohr Siebeck, 2015.

———. "Supersessionism and the Cult Attitude of Stephen and Hebrews." *Irish Theological Quarterly* 89 (2024): 133–50.

Oesterreicher, John M. "*Pro perfidis Judaeis*." *Theological Studies* 8 (1947): 80–96.

O'Malley, John W. *What Happened at Vatican II*. Cambridge, MA: Harvard University Press, 2008.

Overman, J. Andrew. *Matthew's Gospel and Formative Judaism: The Social World of the Matthean Community*. Minneapolis: Fortress Press, 1990.

Paget, J. Carleton. "Jewish Christianity." In *The Cambridge History of Judaism*, 3:731–75. Cambridge: Cambridge University Press, 1999.

Paget, James Carleton. *The Epistle of Barnabas: Outlook and Background*. Wissenschaftliche Untersuchungen zum Neuen Testament 2. Series 64. Tübingen: Mohr Siebeck, 1994.

Passelecq, Georges, and Bernard Suchecky. *The Hidden Encyclical of Pius XI*. 1st U.S. ed., New York: Harcourt Brace, 1997.

Patch, William. "The Catholic Church, the Third Reich, and the Origins of the Cold War: On the Utility and Limitations of Historical Evidence." *The Journal of Modern History* 82 (2010): 396–433.

Paul VI, Pope. *Address of the Holy Father Paul VI: Between the Catholic Church and World Judaism*. January 10, 1975. https://www.vatican.va/content/paul-vi/en/speeches/1975/documents/hf_p-vi_spe_19750110_chiesa-cattolica-ebraismo.html.

Pawlikowski, John T. "Has Antisemitism Been Uprooted from Christianity? A Catholic Response." *Antisemitism Studies* 6 (2022): 241–59.

———. "Religion as Hatred: Antisemitism as a Case Study." *Journal of Hate Studies* 3 (2003–2004): 37–48.

Pearson, Brook W. R., and Stanley E. Porter. *Christian-Jewish Relations through the Centuries*. Journal for the Study of the New Testament Supplements 192. Sheffield, England: Sheffield Academic Press, 2000.

Pius X, Pope. *Lamentabili Sane Exitu*. 1907. https://www.papalencyclicals.net/Pius10/p10lamen.htm.

———. *Pascendi Dominici Gregis*. 1907. https://www.vatican.va/content/pius-x/en/encyclicals/documents/hf_p-x_enc_19070908_pascendi-dominici-gregis.html.

———. *Sacrorum Antistitum*. 1910. https://www.vatican.va/content/pius-x/la/motu_proprio/documents/hf_p-x_motu-proprio_19100901_sacrorum-antistitum.html. English translation https://archive.org/details/sim_american-catholic-quarterly-review_1910-10_35_140/page/712/mode/2up.

Pius XI, Pope. *Divini Redemptoris*. 1937. https://www.vatican.va/content/pius-xi/en/encyclicals/documents/hf_p-xi_enc_19370319_divini-redemptoris.html.

———. *Mit brennender Sorge*. 1937. https://www.vatican.va/content/pius-xi/en/encyclicals/documents/hf_p-xi_enc_14031937_mit-brennender-sorge.html.

Pius XII, Pope. *Divino Afflante Spiritu*. 1943. https://www.vatican.va/content/pius-xii/en/encyclicals/documents/hf_p-xii_enc_30091943_divino-afflante-spiritu.html.

Pontifical Biblical Commission. "The Jewish People and Their Sacred Scriptures in The Christian Bible." 2002. https://www.vatican.va/roman_curia/congregations/cfaith/pcb_documents/rc_con_cfaith_doc_20020212_popolo-ebraico_en.html.

Runesson, Anders. *Judaism for Gentiles: Reading Paul beyond the Parting of the Ways Paradigm*. Wissenschaftliche Untersuchungen zum Neuen Testament 494. Tübingen: Mohr Siebeck, 2022.

Runesson, Anders, and Daniel M. Gurtner, eds. *Matthew within Judaism: Israel and the Nations in the First Gospel*. Atlanta: SBL Press, 2020.

Setzer, Claudia. *Jewish Responses to Early Christians: History and Polemics, 30–150 C.E.* Minneapolis: Fortress Press, 1994.

Schröter, Jens, Benjamin A. Edsall, and Joseph Verheyden, eds. *Jews and Christians—Parting Ways in the First Two Centuries CE: Reflections on the Gains and Losses of a Model*. Beihefte zur Zeitschrift für die neutestamentliche Wissenschaft 253. Berlin: De Gruyter, 2021.

Skarsaune, Oskar. *The Proof from Prophecy: A Study in Justin Martyr's Proof-Text Tradition; Text-Type, Provenance, Theological Profile*. Leiden: Brill. 1988.

Sherwin, Byron L., and Harold Kasimov, eds. *John Paul II and Interreligious Dialogue*. Maryknoll, NY: Orbis Books, 1999.

Sievers, Joseph, and Amy-Jill Levine, eds. *The Pharisees*. Grand Rapids, MI: Eerdmans, 2021.

Simon, Marcel. *Verus Israel: A Study of the Relations between Christians and Jews in the Roman Empire (135–425)*. Oxford: Oxford University Press, 1986.

Soulen, R. Kendall. *The God of Israel and Christian Theology*. Minneapolis, MN: Fortress, 2009.

Stendahl, Krister. "The Apostle Paul and the Introspective Conscience of the West." *The Harvard Theological Review* 56 (1963): 199–215.

Svartvik, Jesper. "'I Have Come Not to Abolish but to Fulfil': Reflections on Understanding Christianity as Fulfilment without Presupposing Supersessionism." *Religions* 13 (2022): 149–59.

———. "Reading the Epistle to the Hebrews without Presupposing Supersessionism." In *Christ Jesus and the Jewish People Today: New Explorations of Theological Relationships*, edited by Philip A. Cunningham, Joseph Sievers, Mary Boys, Hans Hermann Henrix, and Jesper Svartvik, 77–91. Grand Rapids, MI: Eerdmans, 2011.

Tanner, Norman P. *Decrees of the Ecumenical Councils*. 2 vols. Washington, DC: Georgetown University Press, 1990.

Tertullian. *Adversus Marcionem*. Translated by Ernest Evans. Oxford: Clarendon Press, 1972.

Thiessen, Matthew. *A Jewish Paul: The Messiah's Herald to the Gentiles*. Grand Rapids, MI: Baker Academic, 2023.

Trotter, Christine R. *Hellenistic Jews and Consolatory Rhetoric: 2 Maccabees, Wisdom of Solomon, 1 Thessalonians, and Hebrews*. Wissenschaftliche Untersuchungen zum Neuen Testament 2. Series 600. Tübingen: Mohr Siebeck, 2023.

Tucker, J. Brian. *Reading Romans after Supersessionism: The Continuation of Jewish Covenantal Identity*. Eugene, OR: Cascade Books, 2018.

Vorgrimler, Herbert. *Commentary on the Documents of Vatican II*. London: Burns & Oates, 1967.

Williams, A. Lukyn. *Adversus Judaeos: A Bird's-Eye View of Christian Apologetic until the Renaissance*. Cambridge: Cambridge University Press, 1935; digitally printed 2012.

Wolf, Hubert. "The Good Friday Supplication for the Jews and the Roman Curia (1928–1975): A Case Example for Research Projects for the Twentieth Century." In *The Roman Inquisition, the Index and the Jews: Contexts, Sources and Perspectives*, edited by Stephan Wendehorst, 235–57. Boston: Brill, 2004.

Zoccali, Christopher. *Reading Philippians after Supersessionism: Jews, Gentiles, and Covenant Identity*. Eugene, OR: Cascade Books, 2017.

SCRIPTURE INDEX

ANCIENT AUTHORS INDEX

NAME INDEX

GENERAL INDEX